Defeat
INSOMNIA

A Natural Healthcare Guide to Insomnia and
Other Sleep Disorders

By

Monica Jane Shalit and Jeanette Leigh

An imprint of

B. Jain Publishers (P) Ltd.
USA — Europe — India

Disclaimer

Any information given in this book is not intended to be taken as a replacement for medical advice. Any person with a condition requiring medical attention should consult a qualified practitioner or therapist.

DEFEAT INSOMNIA

First Edition: 2012
1st Impression: 2012

All rights reserved. No part of this book may be reproduced, stored in a retrieval system or transmitted, in any form or by any means, mechanical, photocopying, recording or otherwise, without any prior written permission of the publisher.

© 2012 Monica Jane Shalit and Jeanette Leigh

Published by Kuldeep Jain for

An imprint of
B. JAIN PUBLISHERS (P) LTD.
1921/10, Chuna Mandi, Paharganj, New Delhi 110 055 (INDIA)
Tel.: 91-11-4567 1000 • *Fax:* 91-11-4567 1010
Email: info@bjain.com • *Website:* **www.bjain.com**

Printed in India by
JJ Imprints Pvt. Ltd.

ISBN: 978-81-319-0864-8

To

...the billions of people worldwide who cannot get a good night's sleep. Our intention is to help people in their journey towards abundant and sustained health. Without adequate sleep it is a difficult path to negotiate.

Preface

Are you having trouble sleeping through the night?

Do you toss and turn and mull over life's challenges?

Does your bladder act like an alarm clock – several times in the wee small hours?

Are your legs doing a tango while your head tries to waltz into the land of nod?

Does the fact that sleeping is an activity we spend a third of our lives doing, sound excessive and time wasting to you?

If your answer is yes to any of these questions, you may have a sleep problem.

Those who believe that sleep is a passive activity had better read this book and fast because while you slumber your body performs vital functions that restore, heal and regenerate us so that we continue to survive and thrive.

The sleeping brain regulates all of our bodily functions including gastrointestinal, cardiovascular and immune functions. It also processes information and knowledge. Because all this is going on while we are in the land of dreams, we can operate efficiently physically, mentally and emotionally throughout the day. So for the sake of your health it is best not to miss out on sleep.

Rest assured that if you have one of the myriad of sleeping problems you are not alone; millions of people in most countries are just like you. This is because our modern lifestyle is one of the biggest hinderers of sleep.

So many people spend their waking lives experiencing and battling the debilitating effects of too much wakefulness. The purpose of this book is to act as a guide through the maze of ways to deal with sleep issues.

Defeat Insomnia is about taking a holistic approach to your health, so we will be informing you about modalities and remedies that can help you get that evasive good nights' sleep.

We are often stymied by a health condition where we are told by doctors to manage and live with the problem. And we put up with all sorts of pain and discomfort without realising that there are possibly a multitude of helpful alternatives.

If you have been a chronically bad sleeper and the doctor's advice has been to take a sedative, and then you may not have thought about dealing with the root cause of the problem rather than masking it with a drug. Or you might not have the confidence to explore a different approach because you do not know enough about what is available.

Preface

What you will read about in this book will make you say,

'Wow, isn't it fantastic that there are so many ways to prevent as well as manage the inability to sleep properly?'

Investigating new directions means taking on the challenge of really examining your lifestyle and any other issues such as the state of your physical and emotional health. It is our firm belief that this is the way to achieve a more profound healing.

When it comes to sleep, the prognosis is good, and we hope that you are able to take masses of comfort from all the fantastic alternatives that are available.

Now most authors would not say this, but we hope that this book sends you off to sleep.

Jeanette Leigh
Monica Jane Shalit

Acknowledgements

Monica Jane Shalit

Special thanks to John, Dionne and Michail for their loving support and encouragement for all my endeavours. Thanks also to Jeanette for involving me in this project. We have enjoyed 12 months of writing harmoniously together and I look forward to many future projects. I wish to thank my clients who opened up new vistas to me everyday.

Jeanette Leigh

Thanks to my beautiful daughter Laura; our deep sustaining love keeps me healthy, and to her partner, Blessing, for his encouragement. To my co-author and dear friend Monica Jane Shalit, thank you for your great wisdom. Our collaborations are always filled with inspiration and hilarity; we both like to laugh!

Monica and Jeanette both give sincere thanks to naturopaths, Dionne Shalit (B.H.Sc and B.Sc) and Elise Grauer (B.H.Sc) for their invaluable proof reading, discussion and input; Jeanette's dad, artist Ronald Leigh, for his illustrations; Jacqueline Brumley, Iyengar yoga instructor, for her wisdom about yoga asanas, Joanne Callahan for permission to use the information on Thoughtfield Therapy and the Collarbone exercise; and Paul O'Connell, CEO Buteyko Institute for Breathing and Health (International), for his assistance with the Buteyko breathing method.

About the Authors

Monica Jane Shalit, Natural Therapist and Author

Monica Jane Shalit is an internationally renowned complementary therapist. She regards herself as a conduit for lifestyle and attitudinal change.

Monica Jane is a caring, highly regarded health specialist. The modalities she uses include thoughtfield therapy, bioenergetic evaluation, treatment and correction, homoeopathy, flower essences and alchemy. Monica is also a practitioner of Jin Shin Jyutsu, and the organiser of Jin Shin Jyutsu seminars in Australia.

As a sought after public speaker and activist for world peace and the environment, Monica Jane represented the Australian Aborigines at a world peace convention in Switzerland in 1997 and she has worked with indigenous communities around the world such as the Samburu Masai in Kenya. Regular spots on ABC and indigenous radio since 2000 across Australia saw her providing health advice to both aboriginals and non-indigenous Australians.

Her life is dedicated to her family, health, spiritual growth, world peace, animals, and the health of the environment where she has a special interest in Perelandra and biodynamic eco-gardening, as well as the practice of Feng Shui and non violent communication.

Other Publications

'DVT, Deep Vein Thrombosis, The Condition You Don't Have to Have' (Pennon Publishing, 2002) Co-author, Jeanette Leigh.

Jeanette Leigh, Author, Journalist, Blogger

Jeanette Leigh is a journalist, author and passionate believer in the power and importance of the appropriate use of natural therapies. Her first book, *The Natural Health Directory, A Discerning Guide to Leading Medical and Non-Medical Practitioners in Victoria*, was a pioneering work that guided Australians through alternative health approaches.

As an active campaigner for the natural therapies cause, she has produced public and corporate educational health forums and seminars. She is also a sought after public speaker for community groups and on national radio.

Jeanette believes that the search for optimum health is a mental, physical and spiritual journey and that you cannot achieve the best outcomes if you do not have access to all the alternatives.

In addition to her books, Jeanette's work has been featured in national newspapers and magazines as a columnist and feature writer in the areas of health, lifestyle, architecture and design.

Jeanette is a devoted mother and lives in Hawaii.

Other Publications

The Natural Health Directory, A Discerning Guide to Leading Medical and Non-medical Health Practitioners in Victoria (Hill of Content Publishing, 2001).

DVT, Deep Vein Thrombosis, The Condition You Don't Have to Have (Pennon Publishing, 2002), Co-author, Monica Jane Shalit.

Maxine Stripped Naked, Tales From the Sex Industry, (Pennon Publishing, 2004) Biography.

Managing Aches and Pains: A holistic guide to overcoming musculoskeletal complaints and achieving optimal health, (B Jain Publishers Pvt. Ltd. 2010), Co-author, Dr Patrick Mudge.

Introduction

Say Good Night to Sleeplessness

Laugh and the whole world laughs with you
Snore and you sleep alone.

— Anthony Burgess, [Inside Mr Enderby (1963)]

A lot of people think that insomnia simply means not being able to sleep at night, in fact spending the whole night in a state of wakefulness. They do not realise that insomnia encompasses a whole range of sleep challenges.

A staggering 58 per cent of Americans alone suffer from insomnia and millions in the western world are snoring, wriggling and ruminating the night away.

Most people get so used to not sleeping properly and feeling exhausted that they do not realise how big a problem it is.

Sleeping is not an option, it is an essential function. It is as important to our health and well-being as good nutrition. Even while we sleep our body is very, very busy carrying out a myriad of vital tasks.

So, what you will read about in the following pages are all the ways that you can solve the enormous problem of insomnia. Included are remedies and formulas from:

- Naturopathy
- Herbal medicine
- Homoeopathy
- Nutrition
- Ayurveda
- Art therapy
- Flower essences
- Aromatherapy
- Relaxation techniques
- Bath therapies, and
- Some delicious sleep enhancing recipes

So what this book will do is guide you to find the right combination of modes and therapies to persuade your body back to its balanced state for blissful sleep.

Publisher's Note

Insomnia and sleep related disorders are a global epidemic. Defeat Insomnia, authored by Monica Jane Shalit and Jeanette Leigh, is a timely book; a comprehensive insight into the myriad of ways we are sleep challenged.

Filled with a vast range of natural therapy remedies, lifestyle modifications and nourishing slumber inducing recipes, it will be a great resource for your personal library.

Monica and Jeanette inspire and educate people all over the world to make healthy, balanced choices. They remind us that nature is the greatest healer and that we all have the power within ourselves to heal our mind and body. Without a good night's sleep, we will struggle to feel and be well.

We are glad to publish another book written by Jeanette Leigh and to bring natural health expert Monica Jane Shalit into our author list. Working with Jeanette and Monica has been a wonderful experience.

It is our sincere hope that Defeat Insomnia induces you into a balanced sleep that you wake from refreshed and full of vigour to embrace a new day.

Kuldeep Jain
CEO, B. Jain Publishers (P) Ltd.

Contents

Preface .... *v*

Acknowledgements .... *ix*

About the Authors .... *xi*

Introduction .... *xv*

Publisher's Note .... *xvii*

Chapter 1	Sleeping is a Quiet Time for Busyness 1
Chapter 2	Insomnia Explained 5
Chapter 3	The Way We Live and Think, Determines How Well We Sleep 9
Chapter 4	Rediscovering the Art of Sleep 15
Chapter 5	The Brain Drain 19
Chapter 6	Fascinating Rhythms 25

Chapter 7	You are Very, Very Sleepy	39
Chapter 8	Sleep Quiz	43
Chapter 9	The Many Ways in which We Cannot Sleep	47
Chapter 10	Why Many Women Find it Hard to Sleep	65
Chapter 11	Getting Zapped – How Electromagnetic Radiation (EMR) Affects Health and Sleep	79
Chapter 12	Working Nights	87
Chapter 13	Lifestyles of the Tired and Restless	95
Chapter 14	Sleeping during Stressful Times	111
Chapter 15	Natural Therapies Explained	123
Chapter 16	And It's Goodnight From You – Treating Insomnia	127
Chapter 17	Put Away that Laptop and Get to Bed – Children and Sleep	245
Chapter 18	Aging Gracefully – Sleep and the Elderly	253
Chapter 19	Recipes for a Good Nights' Sleep	257
Chapter 20	And It is Good Night from Us	265

CHAPTER 1

Sleeping is a Quiet Time for Busyness

During sleep our brain gets itself organised. It is a bit like defragging a computer; unscrambling all the confusion and restoring all the data in the right compartments. Therefore, having a sleep disorder can have a significant impact on cognitive function, which means your ability to learn and think clearly.

Infants sleep a lot because during that time their brains are developing and making neurological connections to cultivate their intellect, so sleep is crucial for babies. They also need sleep for the growing process.

To a lesser degree sleep is crucial for people of any age as sleep deprivation affects our intellectual and emotional abilities as well as some of our vital bodily functions.

The late Maharishi Mahesh Yogi always said, '*Fatigue is the great enemy.*' However, it is important to identify the enemy in order to find a way to defeat it. So many people are chronically tired, and they think that it is normal and symptomatic of lifestyle, or ageing. And often, because we are so used to reduced levels of functioning we do not even know that we are sleep deprived.

The problem is that sleep deprivation can cause seriously diminished capacities in the following areas:

+ Memory
+ Concentration
+ Creativity
+ Communication and vocabulary
+ Ability to handle complex tasks
+ Decision making
+ Coordination
+ Logical thinking and perception
+ The assimilation and analysis of new information
+ Immunity
+ Healing powers
+ Ability of organs to detoxify

If you want to be a person that functions optimally, a person that can think clearly and make good decisions, a person that does not feel the need to sleep over the course of a day, you need to establish a regular sleep pattern.

How Much We Should Sleep

Joe, on the go

Joe is an alpha male. Life is all go for Joe. He is a financial advisor and his work life is fast paced. Everyday he gets up at 5.30 am, goes to the gym, and then puts in a long day at work. Joe is very driven and feels he has to be on top of and in control of things at all times.

In the evenings he often goes out for a big late dinner with his family. Then he watches television and drinks soft drinks before bedtime. Despite going to the gym in the mornings, Joe is overweight.

Not surprisingly, he suffers from chronic insomnia. He has trouble falling asleep and lies in bed for hours going over the day's events and what he must deal with in the future. If Joe does not make some drastic changes to his lifestyle soon, he is likely to have a physical breakdown of some kind.

***

Imagine being like Joe and using your bed as a think tank. If you consider that a well functioning human being spends around a third of their life in bed (this is equivalent to approximately 24 years if you live to be about 78), then Joe is a long-term sleep-frustrated man.

Being unable to get a proper nights' sleep is not a great scenario when we consider the vital functions that our body performs during this period such as regulating hormones and stabilising blood sugar. The consequences of sleep deprivation are very serious, and in the long term, they can even be the cause of accidents.

The nature of sleep varies according to our age as does the proportion of sleep devoted to the various sleep stages. During these stages the body performs restorative activities that are not carried out during the day.

Infants spend half of their sleep time in stage 5, the Rapid Eye Movement (REM) stage, which is the deep stage of sleep (more about that later), whereas adults only spend 20 per cent of their slumbering in this phase.

During the deep sleep phase growth hormone are released, which is why children and teenagers require so much sleep.

The following Table 1.1 sets out the amount of sleep that people need during each stage of their lives:

Table 1.1

Age	Amount of Sleep
Babies 1-2 months	15-20 hours
Infants 3-11 months	9-12 hours at night plus sleeps of between 30 minutes and 2 hours, 1-4 times a day
Toddlers 1-3 years	12-14 hours
Children 3-5 years (preschool)	11-13 hours
Children 5-12 years (school)	10-11 hours
Teenagers 11-17 (secondary school)	8.5-9.25 hours
Adults	7-9 hours
Older adults	6-8 hours

Chapter 2

Insomnia Explained

Lots of people think that insomnia means being completely sleepless, where a person lies awake all night unable to relinquish consciousness. This is true in extreme cases but insomnia comes in a variety of guises accompanied by a multitude of symptoms:

- ✦ Difficulty falling asleep
- ✦ Inability to stay asleep
- ✦ Waking up too early in the morning
- ✦ Not feeling rested after a night's sleep

Put simply, insomnia is a sleep disorder. However, researchers have identified more than 80 types of sleep disorders that rest under this definition. People develop insomnia of whatever kind for a lot of different reasons because we all have different life experiences.

It is important to realise that rarely is insomnia a life sentence however it can be temporary, intermittent or chronic.

Temporary, lasting for a short period of time due to a particular stressor such as noisy neighbours, relationship upsets or hot weather

Intermittent, happening occasionally; for instance, someone who travels regularly and has their body clock disrupted, or if a person has regular stressful periods at work

Chronic, which is when a person cannot sleep most or all nights

Likely Candidates

Causes of sleeplessness are many and varied. Insomnia can develop due to ill health, electromagnetic radiation, jet lag, physiological, psychological and hormonal problems, stress or food allergies. Women are more likely candidates than men for a variety of reasons. The elderly and depressed are also more susceptible.

It is relatively common for people to experience insomnia at one time or another (it affects around 1 in 5 people) as we journey through life and experience different challenges and stressors. However, eventually normal sleep patterns return. Where we run into trouble is when a pattern of disrupted sleep or sleep deprivation sets in on a regular basis for any number of reasons. These can include:

- ✦ Pharmaceutical medications such as anti-hypertensive drugs, weight loss agents, pseudoephedrine, the oral contraceptive pill, corticosteroids (for inflammatory conditions), drugs to treat Parkinson's disease and anti-depressants can all cause sleeplessness

- Sleeping pills or sedative and hypnotic pharmaceutical drugs such as benzodiazepines, which are prescribed to induce sleep in people with chronic and long term insomnia, may in fact produce tolerance to the sedative effect and perpetuate chronic insomnia
- Recreational drug use
- Nicotine
- Substances found in tea, coffee, cocoa and cola drinks such as caffeine, theobromine and theophylline, which are types of methylxanthine, a stimulant
- Alcohol accelerates the onset of sleep, decreases the period of time spent in REM and causes sleep disturbance in the second half of the sleep period
- Poor lifestyle habits, otherwise known as sleep hygiene, is one of the biggest culprits when it comes to sleep problems. This involves the habits you develop in relation to sleep

If you do not even have time to say good night to your pillow...

If you fall asleep as soon as your head hits the pillow, make no mistake, you are sleep deprived. Under normal circumstances it takes around 15-20 minutes to fall asleep as our body starts to wind down into a soporific state.

Chapter 3

The Way We Live and Think, Determines How Well We Sleep

The current state of the planet, suffering from global warming and climate change, has sent nations into a flurry of activity to try and halt the damage. While they are trying to develop new or modified technology to do this, they are overlooking one important element that could save us from destruction that is returning to the source of the problem, which is our disconnection with our true selves and nature.

Luckily, there is a simple answer to this problem which is to fall back in love with our self.

This might seem simplistic, however, if we truly love ourselves then we will only want to nurture ourselves in every possible way by:

- Nourishing ourselves with good natural unprocessed food
- Being conscious and aware of everything that we do, feel and think and say
- Having lots of fun and laughter
- Loving without conditions
- Valuing everything we do
- Feeling and maintaining the rhythms of life; including the sleep and circadian cycle
- Re-establishing a connection with nature
- Not behaving in ways that are destructive towards ourselves, others or the planet

How many of us can say we truly love ourselves like that?

Our lifestyles are a major contributor to poor sleep patterns. We are busy, wound up and stressed, with a less than optimum work/leisure balance.

It was reported in an Australian newspaper* that more than two million Australians work more than 50 hours a week. If you think about it, the way we live today actually dictates that we sacrifice sleep to create extra time for work and leisure.

We actually want to party all night, get drunk and feel terrible the next day. We even wear such an experience as a badge of honour and relish retelling the story to our mates.

And we actually feel compelled by employers and market forces to work 12-16 hours a day, often. Strange huh?

---

*Herald Sun newspaper, October 2009.

The problem is that our sleep debts are a significant stressor with many serious repercussions.

Sick and Tired

Ill health is chronic in most countries. In fact, populations are 100 times sicker than their ancestors of 100 years ago. Illness disrupts sleep, which can cause a vicious cycle because we need sleep to help us heal.

Poor health affects everything, including economies. Research studies undertaken across Europe and America show that economic gains are significantly impacted by the health of the nation. A study of economic growth in the United Kingdom between 1790 and 1980 revealed that the economy improved by 30 per cent due to better health and diet. The same figure applies to a study conducted in 10 industrialised countries up to the mid-1990s. Obviously, if we are sick we are unable to work effectively or at all.

Increased levels of sickness are largely due to our lifestyles and most illness could be avoided by changing the way we eat and live. If we want things to be different we have to ask ourselves what it takes to have good health.

The Vedic scriptures say, – *'Disease never comes without a cause. The way is prepared, and disease invited, by disregard of the laws of health and of nature.'*

The reality is that under current circumstances we are unlikely to be disease free because the kind of life we desire perpetuates the toxicity of the environment and this is what we absorb.

People with Near Perfect Health

The Hunza population, who lived an isolated life at the foothills of the Himalayas in north-east Pakistan, is often held up as an example of an almost disease free society. (Although now it is reported that 'civilisation' is creeping in there and changing that state of being.) Generally, many people in the population were reported to live to well over a hundred years old.

A British surgeon, Dr Robert McCarrison, carried out extensive nutritional research in the early twentieth century on the Indian subcontinent. He spent much time with the Hunza population and this is what he discovered:

- A population that was warm, friendly and religious with a tremendous sense of community
- People with near perfect physical and mental health; there were no signs of cancer, heart disease, diabetes, ulcers, colitis, diverticulosis, high blood pressure, childhood ailments and teeth were healthy and free of dental caries
- There were no doctors or hospitals in the vicinity
- There was no juvenile delinquency or crime and no police or jails
- People respected their elders
- Men were fathering children when they were 100 years old and some people lived beyond 150
- Women experienced no problems during childbirth
- Childhood diseases were hardly known
- Women of 80 looked 40
- People generally had unblemished complexions and looked young
- They were gentle, good natured people

The Hunzas lived in a harsh climate and worked hard. They played sport and drank water that was mineralised. They ate much of their fruits and vegetables raw and the kernels and seeds of their fruit. Their diet consisted of legumes, whole grain food, goats' cheese and butter. Their consumption of meat and dairy products was low and crops were grown with mineralised water.

Getting Ratty

Dr McCarrison understood that the diet and lifestyle of these people had a major effect on their emotional and physical health. He set out to prove it to the post-industrial world by carrying out some ground breaking tests of the effects of diet on rats.

He set up three control groups of rats. One group was fed the staple Hunza diet, one was fed what the poor of Bengal and Madras ate that is, some pulses, rice, old vegetables, a little bit of milk and city water, and a third group were fed what the working class Englishman of the day ate, which was refined white bread, sugar, margarine, sweet tea, boiled vegetables, tinned meat and jam.

Results

Bengal/Madras Diet: These rats developed a long list of diseases including ear, nose, throat, lungs and upper respiratory illness, gastrointestinal illnesses, skin diseases, reproductive problems, cancers of the blood and lymph glands, heart disease and oedema.

Working Class Englishman's Diet: The same litany of diseases developed; however their complications and severity were greater. In addition, they displayed pronounced delinquency, biting and cannibalism.

Hunza Diet: These rats maintained their robustness and health.

Dr McCarrison's findings demonstrated that many common diseases that were prevalent in industrial societies were caused simply by extensive food processing; the use of refined white flour and chemical additives being a case in point.

The conclusion is clear; nothing produces ill health like bad food. And yet despite the fact that we all have access to this information, populations continue to manufacture and eat refined, highly processed, chemicalised foods that adversely affect our emotions, social behaviour and physical health.

It is interesting and perhaps appalling to note that Dr McCarrison's definitive work was largely ignored by the medical profession and governments.

Lifestyles of the Sick and Exhausted

Clearly fast food, fast lives and technology continue to make us sick and unable to sleep adequately. Having our engine/body rev constantly without adequate food and rest means we run the risk of breaking down; and our body begins to run on empty. We feel tired and tense throughout the day, which further perpetuates the cycle of sleeplessness. We even get so used to feeling exhausted that we think it is normal.

Sleep deficits affect not only our ability to learn and our memory; they significantly impact hormone levels, weight, mood and metabolic processes.

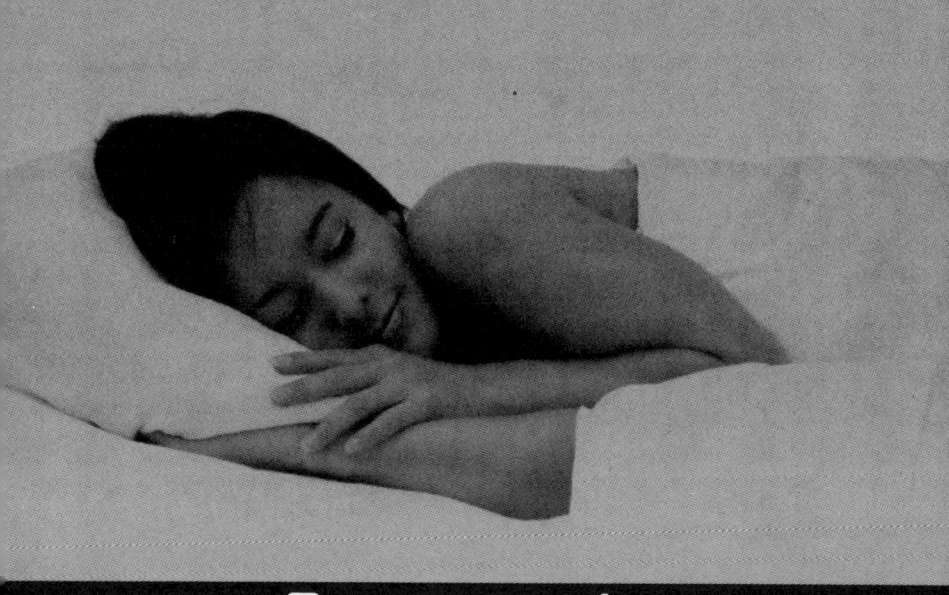

Chapter 4

Rediscovering the Art of Sleep

There is no single way to rectify a sleep disorder, but first you need to understand why you cannot sleep properly. This enables you to look for the right combination of solutions.

It is very unlikely that you will solve your sleep issues with just one magic cure. For instance, if you cannot sleep because you have a stressful job then you will need to approach insomnia from a number of perspectives. Firstly it would be important to deal with the way you think and feel about your work and devise a strategy to cope with the stressors.

Secondly, regardless of what unfolds during the day, there are many ways to achieve a relaxed state before bed time to help re-establish a sleep routine. This might involve a combination of modalities such as aromatherapy, having a bath and meditating. Sometimes a stronger approach is needed such as a course of herbal treatment and lifestyle modifications. This book sets out many alternatives.

It is important to note that we should not approach any health issues without addressing emotions, lifestyle and possibly physiological issues.

So, to relearn the art of sleeping soundly, read on.

How a Good Night's Sleep Feels – In Case you have Forgotten

A good night's sleep leaves us feeling restored, grounded, balanced, focused and connected. We have good energy to allow us to cope with all that the day brings. Our memory is acute and our attention fully present.

To help you achieve this, we are going to take you on a journey of understanding that will stimulate you to seek your own sleep solutions. You will learn about how sleep works and what happens in each stage. From this you will discover how important it is to have the right amount of sleep at the right time of night.

Knowledge gives us the power to look after ourselves appropriately. In order to heal or redress the causes of our physical, mental and emotional imbalances we need to take control of our health. How many of you go to a health practitioner and come out not really understanding what is wrong with you, why you have the condition and how the medications work?

Achieving and maintaining good health means being discerning about the approach we take, and the practitioners we engage to assist us. We also need to understand the different kinds of modalities and their effects, for instance, how long it will take for a herb to take effect and how a particular physical therapy works.

We have the best chance of good health if we are active participants in the healing process.

Slumbering and Functioning

This might seem contradictory, but although we are in a state of inertia and rest, a sleeping brain is incredibly active. It continues to regulate all our bodily functions including gastrointestinal, cardiovascular and immune functions as well as cognitive processing.

Most of our detoxification is carried out by our detoxification factories, the kidneys and liver, during the night while we sleep. Therefore a lack of sleep can significantly weaken the body's ability to rid itself of waste. Rich fatty, fried and spicy foods, as well as alcohol and caffeine can impair our ability to sleep well because they severely affect the liver.

The liver is the most active processing centre. When any substance enters the body via ingestion or through application to the skin, be they good or toxic products, the liver receives them first. It metabolises and either packages and stores them, ships them out for use by other organs, or sends them off to be excreted.

The liver stores most vitamins and many minerals, including zinc. It is involved in the functioning of the immune and endocrine systems, which includes sex and stress hormones. The liver also clears hormones that have done their job. A healthy liver means a better hormone balance and stable blood sugar level.

However, the liver has an added level of significance; it is not just a centre for detoxification, it can also be viewed from a spiritual perspective. There is a belief that the liver is the seat of the soul, and where the soul is anchored. So, when we sleep the liver becomes the soul's bridge between the spiritual realms and the earth. It anchors us in our bodies as we dream.

Therefore strong, healthy organs will support body and soul, enabling peaceful sleep.

A complex variety of functions are performed while we sleep, which allows us to operate physically, mentally and emotionally throughout the day.

Sleep quality also depends on the following factors:

- Amount of hours slept
- Time of going to sleep
- Amount of time spent awake
- Daytime activities

Sleep and wakefulness are inextricably linked because they are a part of the same function. Anything that disturbs sleep will disturb wakefulness and vice versa.

Because sleep and wakefulness cannot be separated, the treatment of some sleep disorders involves changing what a person does during the day so that they sleep better at night. For example, catching 40 winks in the afternoon can disrupt the night time sleep cycle. In fact, if you want to sleep at night you have to begin preparation early in the morning because what you do, take, feel and think during the day impacts sleep.

For those who are predisposed to chronic insomnia, such as people suffering from serious or chronic illnesses, sleeplessness can turn into an insomnia cycle that is hard to break.

In this instance bedtime can become associated with worry about not sleeping rather than a pleasant regenerative process. This can result in a cycle of anxiety and fear around sleep so the more a person tries to sleep the more difficult it becomes. But do not worry; if this scenario applies to you there are a number of ways to help break the cycle.

CHAPTER 5

The Brain Drain

No Sleep Makes Us Sluggish, Poor and Unwise

Because the demands of daily life drain us physically and mentally, we need rest time to regroup and rejuvenate. This is why we sleep.

Normal cognitive skills such as speech, memory and innovative and flexible thinking are restored and reorganised during sleep's various stages.

Research shows that sleep plays a significant role in brain development. If we do not sleep our brain becomes sluggish. You will know this feeling if you have been a university student who has had to stay up all night to finish an assignment, or if you have partied all night. The next day you feel groggy and irritable and have trouble remembering even basic things. It is difficult to concentrate and your attention span is like that of an insect.

If You Think You Can Live without Sleep, Dream on

Being awake for 17 consecutive hours is equivalent to the impairment caused by drinking two glasses of wine (blood alcohol level of .05 per cent, the legal drink driving limit in Australia and England).

What we know is that if sleep evades us regularly it actually affects the part of the brain controlling language, memory and sense of time. If a person is sufficiently sleep deprived those faculties can almost cease to function.

Deep sleep also has a profound effect on our mental state. Research has shown that the parts of the brain that control emotions, decision making and social interactions appear to be quiet during deep sleep. This suggests that they are using that time to recover from all the hard work they do during wakefulness.

Sleep deprivation can have dire consequences. History shows that people deprived of sleep often find it difficult to respond quickly to situations and make rational decisions.

It is believed that sleep deprivation contributed to disasters such as the Challenger shuttle explosion, the Exxon Valdezspill, the nuclear disaster at Chernobyl and the melting of the nuclear reactor core at Three Mile Island. In fact, tiredness is responsible for around 25 per cent of road accidents, loss of productivity in the work place and even marriage and relationship breakdowns.

So it is in everybody's interest that we all get a good night's sleep!

Investigating the Deep

Professor Robert Stickgold, a cognitive neuroscientist, has conducted many research studies into sleep and the effects of sleep deprivation. His studies show that a crucial function of sleep is to boost memory and learning; that during sleep, the brain evaluates information that has been recently learnt and consolidates, stabilises and organises memories and skills that have been acquired during our waking hours.

During each of the five stages of sleep different functions occur that get our thoughts organised, filed and consolidated.

Experiments suggest that:

+ REM stage is crucial for reorganising and cross-referencing memories
+ Non-REM sleep is involved in reinforcing memories

Let's Sleep on it

We know what it is to sleep on a problem and wake up in the morning with an answer that has been evading us. That is because sleep may also facilitate more complex forms of insight.

A study conducted in 2004 surveyed a group of subjects in Germany who were asked to work on a series of interrelated mathematical problems containing a hidden rule that allowed the problems to be solved more quickly.

Those who returned to the puzzles after a nights' sleep found the shortcut approximately twice as often as those who had spent an equal amount of time on the problem while awake.

Researchers suggested that the insight was enabled because the memory was restructuring the information during sleep.

Old before Your Time

Have you heard of anti-ageing medicine? If you have then you will know that it is not about wrinkle creams, botox injections or plastic surgery. It is about maintaining youthfulness through good health and healthy attitudes towards life.

An important contributor to staying young is having the right amount of sleep at the right time.

Research has shown that if you develop chronic sleeplessness it effects hormone production and metabolism to the point where it has a similar effect on the ageing process, hence the development of a range of age related illnesses such as loss of memory, type 2 diabetes and high blood pressure.

The research published in the medical journal 'The Lancet' (October 23, 1999; 354:1435-1439) showed that on returning to normal sleep patterns, blood sugar and hormone concentrations normalised.

Other consequences of chronic sleep loss revealed through the study included:

- ✦ Blood sugar levels of male participants took 40 per cent longer to drop following a high carbohydrate meal, compared with the sleep-recovery period
- ✦ There was a 30 per cent drop in the subjects' insulin responses, which is similar to the effects of insulin resistance and a precursor to type 2 diabetes
- ✦ Sleep-deprived men had raised cortisol (stress hormone) levels similar to those seen in older people. This may be involved in insulin resistance and memory loss related to age

For adults, tissue cells that are worn out through the normal wear and tear of living require sleep to repair. When you do not get enough good quality sleep, your vital organs and other tissues are not getting the vital repair and hormones they need for the restoration.

Sleepless in America, Europe, Asia, Australia

It is staggering to think that more than 40 million Americans suffer from chronic sleep disorders. Billions of dollars are spent each year on sleeping pills. In India, over 125 million people suffer from insomnia and in Australia nearly 2.5 million.

Sleep Deprivation is Costly

A study conducted by Access Economics, an Australian economic consulting firm, completed in 2004 estimated that more than 1.2 million Australians (6 per cent of the population) experienced sleep disorders, which cost the nation $10.3 billion in 2004.

Sleep disorders contribute to a range of other health and social problems, and this has substantial health and economic impacts from accidents, injuries, chronic illnesses and production and consumption losses.

The study found that sleep disorders are responsible for:
- 9.1 per cent of work-related injuries
- 8.3 per cent of depression
- 7.6 per cent of non work-related motor vehicle accidents
- 2.9 per cent of diabetes
- 0.9 per cent of nephritis and nephrosis (kidney disease)
- 0.6 per cent of cardiovascular disease[*]

---

[*]Figures are taken from, *'Wake Up Australia: The Value of Healthy Sleep'*, Report by Access Economics Pvt Ltd for Sleep Health, Australia.

For Australia alone the financial costs of sleep disorders were $200 million in 2004.

Sleep is not an optional enterprise. Most mammals, birds, reptiles and bugs do it. Rats deprived of sleep apparently die faster than those deprived of food.

Disorders such as sleep apnoea, which results in excessive daytime sleepiness, have been linked to stress and high blood pressure.

Chapter 6

Fascinating Rhythms

When it comes to sleep, Benjamin Franklin knew what he was talking about:

Early to bed early to rise makes a man healthy, wealthy and wise.

The Sleep Cycle

The sleep cycle consists of five stages; stages 1, 2, 3 and 4 are known as the non-rapid eye movement periods (NREM), and the fifth stage is the rapid eye movement stage or REM. You move through the five stages throughout the night and one cycle takes between 90-110 minutes. It is so important to go to sleep

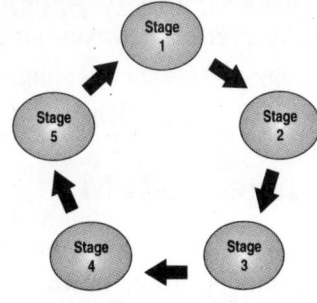

Fig. 6.1 *The Sleep Cycle*

when you are tired because if you do not you will miss out on the 90 minute cycle and it will take another 90 minutes to go to sleep.

Stage 1 NREM

The first stage of sleep is light in nature. It is the transition period between being awake and asleep so we may drift in and out of sleep easily. Our body is relaxed and our eyes closed. Eye and muscle activity slows and we often have brief, fleeting thoughts. It is during this time that people may experience muscle contractions, which can cause that peculiar feeling of falling. Stage 1 usually lasts 1-7 minutes.

Stage 2 NREM

This stage begins as soon as we fall asleep. Eye movement stops and brain waves slow down. It is a period of light sleep where the body's relaxation progresses and fragments of dreams may be experienced. Stage 2 usually lasts between 10-20 minutes.

Stage 3 NREM

This is a transitional stage of sleep and the first stage of deep sleep, which is moderately deep. The body's temperature and blood pressure begin to decrease and skeletal muscles become completely relaxed. Slow and fast brain waves combine. If you have ever been woken up during this stage you will know that groggy disoriented feeling. It is hard to wake someone up during stage 3 sleep, which lasts between 15 and 30 minutes.

Stage 4 NREM

During stage 4, the brain is in the deepest stage of sleep and brain activity is slowed down considerably. At this time we are almost exclusively producing slow brain waves. It is also hard to wake a person in this period. Without stages 3 and 4 sleep, you will not wake up feeling refreshed and restored. Those who sleep walk or wet the bed will do so in this period of sleep. Stage 4 lasts between 15-30 minutes.

Stage 5 REM

Most of our dreams, and vivid ones at that, happen during REM sleep. Brain activity is heightened, blood pressure and heart rate increase and breathing is faster as well as irregular and shallow. Eyes move rapidly and muscles become immobile. This stage is still not wholly understood but it is believed that it is a time when long term memories are formed.

***

Vital functions occur in each stage of sleep. Studies, conducted by the University of Warwick, and University College London, of one million adults have shown that lack of sleep can double the risk of death from cardiovascular disease and conversely too much sleep can have the same effect.

If a person experiences patchy sleep for a short period of time they are at risk of performing their work and other activities poorly. If this situation goes on for an extended period, such as with shift workers who sleep in stages throughout a day and night, it can cause and contribute to deterioration of vital cognitive and physical functions.

Dream On ...

Some dreams are divinely inspired and others are the direct result of the physical body.

– Hippocrates
(Ancient Greek physician and Father of modern medicine)

So far you have read about how damaging the lack of sleep can be physiologically, however we must also consider the mental and emotional repercussions. If we do not sleep properly then we do not dream properly, or at all. Dreaming is another important function of our subconscious.

We all do it whether we are aware of it or not. Babies dream up to eight hours a night and adults for approximately two hours.

Our brain has two hemispheres, left and right. The left brain is our logical, rational and analytic side and the right is intuitive and creative. This is the hemisphere that is more active when we are sleeping and dreaming.

Dreams are a language filled with symbols and metaphor and as such they can be used as tools to understand the unconscious mind or how we tick.

During the NREM period we can experience dreams about recent life episodes, however, sometimes remote memories will appear as well.

Most of our dreams occur during REM sleep. This is the time when our brain is highly active and our blood pressure rises, however the muscle tone is diminished and we are rendered immobile. There is a disorder called REM sleep behaviour disorder where the REM 'paralysis' does not occur and the person physically acts out their dreams. This can be intense and dangerous, especially if you are having a nightmare.

During the REM period, dreams are lucid and filled with intense and vivid imagery. In fact, a dream can be so vivid that for a period of time we think it is real. A person may even recognise that they are dreaming.

'Lucid' dreams can also be frightening, disturbing, happy, uplifting, colourful or monochrome. We can even smell things during a dream.

The parade of images and events that pass through our sleeping brain tell us stories. Even though they are often weird and bizarre, they are rich in meaning.

Considering that we spend a third of our lives sleeping, we do a lot of dreaming and hence a lot of mental and emotional processing during sleep. This processing can be likened to the body's physiological detoxification function. While we sleep the body filters and eliminates toxins through the kidneys, liver and skin. Likewise dreams are a clearing centre for our psyche, or subconscious mind.

Dreams help us:

- Clear and heal emotions
- Solve problems
- Remember that there are emotional issues to be sorted out
- Reflect what we are thinking and feeling
- Understand and process our daily experiences
- Maintain mental health
- Be prophetic-you may have experienced dreaming about someone you have not seen for a long time and then you suddenly hear from them or run into them somewhere

Nightmares are as important as pleasant dreams. Bad dreams can adversely affect our mental predisposition during the day. However, to acknowledge and consider the messages the dream holds is important because it can be a key to healing some hurt or trauma. So dreams can be cathartic.

Unexpressed emotions that sit below the surface of our consciousness can manifest themselves in dreams, which gives us the opportunity to clear them. Dreams can also alert us to our own physical problems, rehearse us to deal with personal challenges, allow experimental thoughts and provide insights and creative solutions. It is a complex function and the imagery is cloaked in many guises causing strong emotional responses.

If we do not deal with our emotional issues in some way they can eventually manifest as physical illness. Think about the metaphor of illness and pain. A sore throat could be the result of something we need to say to someone but cannot due to fear.

A pain in the back could be the result of feeling unsupported and lacking in money. Hurting a leg or foot could represent an inability to walk forward in life. Breast disease can be about a lack of self nurturance. The shoulders are the 'shoulds', people who feel that they 'should' always do the right thing and be responsible. These are just general examples to give an idea of how to apply this thinking.

The quality of sleep affects our dreaming and our dreams can affect the quality of our sleep. If someone is depressed and going through a tough time they may either not dream, therefore they are not processing their emotions and could manifest physical illness, or they may have distressing dreams, which disrupt sleep and make us wake unrefreshed.

Theories abound about dreams and their purpose and it is a fascinating topic that is worth exploring because they can tell you a lot about yourself and assist in a healing process. By appropriately processing your emotions you reduce stress and increase emotional, spiritual and physical health. Dreams are another medium to address problems.

If you are interested in further understanding your dreams you can keep a journal and observe patterns and explore your own thought processes.

Tick Tock goes the Body's Clock

Almost all other animals are observed to partake of sleep; aquatic, winged and terrestrial creatures alike. For every kind of fish and the soft shelled species have been seen sleeping, as has every other creature that has eyes.

– Aristotle (384-322 BC)

Our bodies perform complex chemical routines every moment of our lives. Many of our bodily functions, both in humans and animals, are regulated by biological rhythms.

At one end of the scale there's the very long winter sleep known as hibernation, which helps animals such as bears and squirrels survive harsh seasons devoid of food sources. At the other end, there is the daily routine that most creatures indulge in known as sleep and wakefulness.

Prior to electricity, humans were ruled by the waning and rising of the sun to determine sleep times. Electricity brought artificial light, which affected sleep patterns significantly.

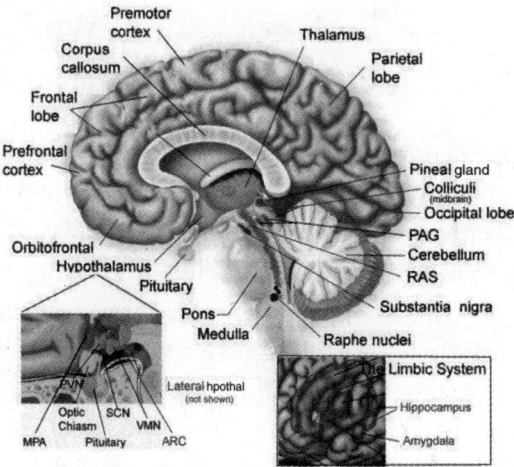

Fig. 6.2 *Function Centres of the Brain*

Light and Darkness Cycle

The rhythms of life are logical and the goal is nurturance and growth. Sunrise alerts us that the day is beginning and stimulates the waking centre in the brain. This interaction tunes the body to wakefulness when it is light and to slumber when it is dark. This is known as the circadian rhythm or body clock and it has evolved over many lifetimes, aligning human physiology with the environment.

The term circadian comes from the Latin word 'circa', meaning around, and 'diem' or 'dies', meaning day. It describes a 24 hour biochemical, physiological and behavioural cycle. The circadian rhythm governs all living creatures be they plant, animal, fungal, bacterial or human.

Circadian rhythms determine our daily cycle from sleep to wakefulness by alternately inhibiting and exciting different parts of the brain through regulating the release of chemicals called neurotransmitters such as serotonin.

Tock Tick goes a Skewed Biochemistry Clock

If we are deprived of sufficient sleep and act contrary to the body's rhythms, such as eating meals when the body clock expects it to be sleep time, or sleeping during the day, it will cause conflicting signals to fly around the brain.

Your body will be alerted to produce sleep chemicals at times when you need to be awake and alert, and chemicals for wakefulness when it is time for rest. This makes us feel confused and at the very least we feel out of sorts. Those who have experienced jet lag or shift work through the night will understand this feeling all too well.

Much of the sleep story is about chemicals, and this is how they work:

+ The main biochemical cause of insomnia is the body's failure to produce enough melatonin, which is the chemical that induces sleep when it is dark
+ Melatonin is produced in the pineal gland from serotonin, and serotonin is derived from tryptophan, an amino acid that we get from certain foods

So the important pathway to sleep is paved with:

Tryptophan, which becomes serotonin, which becomes melatonin

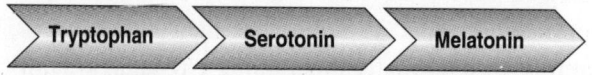

Fig. 6.3 *The Chemical Pathway to Sleep*

Melatonin production can be easily disrupted just by switching on a light. So if you go to the bathroom at night, try to do so in relative darkness; of course taking care not to bump into anything.

If a person is unable to sleep properly due to excitement or stress they produce stress hormones such as adrenaline and cortisol that can interfere with the synthesis of the neurotransmitter serotonin. (Serotonin also helps to regulate mood.)

Producing the Right Chemicals Naturally

Now, these chemicals do not just happen without some outside help. We cause our body to produce serotonin from tryptophan by the intake of certain vitamins and minerals; specifically vitamin B6 (pyridoxine), magnesium and vitamin D from the sun. These are essential for converting each other ultimately into melatonin, without which, we will not be able to sleep.

A serotonin imbalance can also be responsible for endogenous depression, which is a depression caused by chemical imbalance. So people suffering from this kind of depression will often suffer from insomnia.

Remember, When?

Recent ground breaking research conducted on Siberian hamsters revealed that a functioning circadian system is critical to a hamsters' ability to remember what they have learned. Without it, in fact, they cannot remember anything.

Biologists report that hamsters with disabled circadian systems consistently failed to remember their environment, unlike their kin folk with normally functioning circadian systems.

Hamsters with their circadian rhythms surgically removed could not remember their normal environment or anything that they had recently learnt.

This is the first time that it has been scientifically demonstrated that the circadian rhythm is critical to the functioning of learning and memory.

Clocking in

For some must watch while some must sleep
Thus runs the world away.

– William Shakespeare (1601)

The biological clock is a vital regulator situated in a part of the brain called the suprachiasmatic nucleus, located near the sleep/wake centre.

If your internal time keeper is not functioning properly, there are many consequences.

The big ben of the brain

- ✦ The suprachiasmatic nucleus (the circadian centre of the brain) is like a master clock which has an internal timer of approximately 24 hours. This area of the brain also regulates our emotions, memory and concentration so it is not surprising that disruption of our sleep and waking functions are often associated with our mood and concentration

Running low on memory

- ✦ A dodgy body clock can cause the release of too much of a neurotransmitter called gamma-amino butyric acid (GABA). Studies show that an excess of GABA inhibits the brain in a way that leads to short term memory problems and the inability to retain new information

A hippo is not just a large beast that yawns a lot

- ✦ Another part of the brain known as the hippocampus, needs to be stimulated in order for the things you learn to be organised in such a way that you will remember them later. It is believed that the hippocampus is responsible for the formation of new memories and placing them in the long term memory for later retrieval

Remembering ... um something

- ✦ A study undertaken at Stanford University revealed that the circadian system, or internal body clock, must be in optimal condition in order for you to learn new information and remember it

For the term of an unnatural life

- It is believed that disruptions to the body clock over many years through insomnia or night shift work can impact longevity to the point where a person can lessen their lifespan by ten or more years
- Each individual's circadian rhythm regulates activity throughout the body, including the brain, lungs, heart, liver and skeletal muscles. The internal clock keeps all the organs and systems running smoothly

Heavy news

- A body clock in disrepair is a 'fat load of good' because it can adversely affect health in so many ways; it can even make you obese
- Research shows that sleep deficiency may increase the risk of obesity because chemicals and hormones that play a key role in controlling appetite and eating behaviour are released during sleep
- The two hormones in question are leptin and ghrelin. On the one hand, the body decreases its production of leptin, which is the hormone that tells your brain that you do not need any more food and that it has stored sufficient fat. At the same time it increases its levels of ghrelin, a hormone that triggers hunger. No wonder a sleep deprived person makes a 'b' line for the fridge.

Having the right amount of good quality sleep at the appropriate time will assist your circadian clock to function like clockwork.

Peace, Brown Rice and a Good Night's Sleep

You may think you are doing all the right things to maintain good health. However, if you do not sleep well and regularly, the body loses its equilibrium and all the benefits of organic food and exercise may be negated.

For instance, studies have shown a correlation between sleep and the release of chemicals called cytokines, which activate an immune or inflammatory response. What is being increasingly understood is that inflammation is the cause of many chronic diseases such as cardiovascular disease, arthritis, autoimmune diseases and cancer.

A study published in February 2009 in the journal *Sleep* showed that the less we sleep, the more cytokines we produce. These cytokines help regulate inflammation and the more they are produced, the greater the inflammation. So, an inflammatory process is fostered because of lack of sleep.

The researchers also linked reduced sleep duration with an increased risk of death because sleep deprived people are at greater risk of developing illnesses such as coronary heart disease, diabetes and obesity.

And the vicious cycle continues as poor sleep can also perpetuate chronic illness and pain.

Following are some of the physical conditions that can cause insomnia:

- Arthritis, due to pain
- Kidney disease
- Heart failure

- Asthma
- Sleep apnoea
- Narcolepsy
- Restless leg syndrome
- Parkinson's disease
- Hyperthyroidism
- Depression

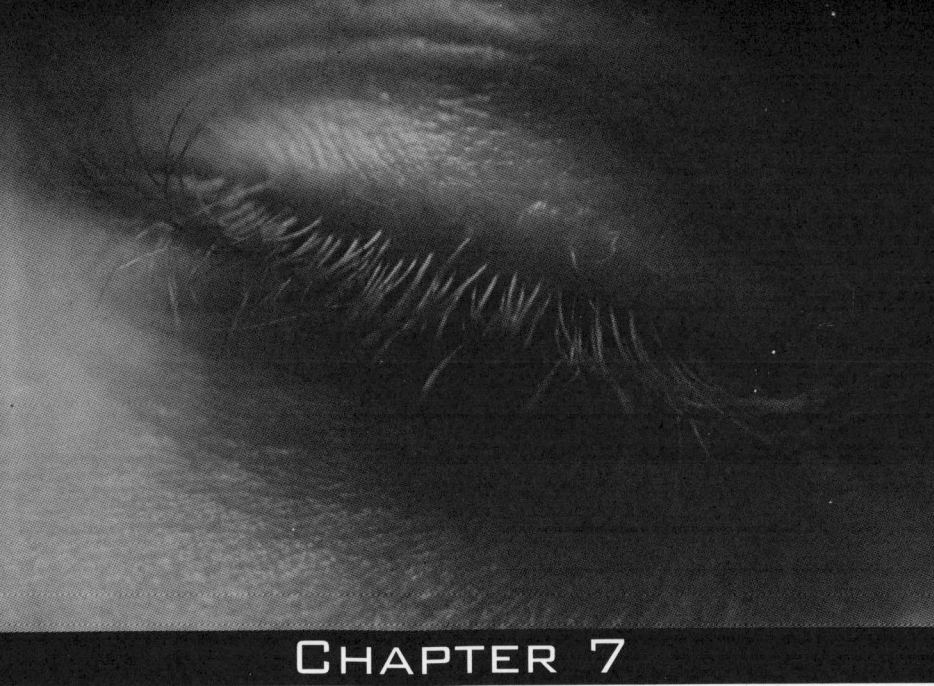

Chapter 7

You are Very, Very Sleepy

Now that you know what happens when you do not sleep, I am sure you want to get on and solve your sleep issues.

Often people are perplexed about what to do when faced with sleep problems and a doctor will more than likely suggest a pharmaceutical solution. Western medicine uses a variety of drugs to treat insomnia. Sedatives or hypnotics with names ending in '…pine' and '…pam' can relieve the symptoms of insomnia, but they can be addictive and they do not get to the heart of the matter, that is, why you are not sleeping. They provide only a short-term result that lasts for as long as the medicine is taken.

Understanding the reason why the sleeping challenge has come about gives us the opportunity to actually solve it rather than mask it with pharmaceuticals.

Ill-health does not necessarily begin with a physiological cause. In order to understand why we are out of sorts, unsettled or unwell we need to examine everything about ourselves and our lives including emotions, lifestyle, physical being and spirit.

All of us are the sum of a whole lot of elements so returning to a healthy, well-rested self requires a balance of all of them.

Balance in all Things

This book approaches insomnia from a 'natural therapy' point of view because it focuses on returning the overall functioning of an individual to a balanced state (homoeostasis). However, not all modalities may be capable of doing that in and of themselves. A combination of approaches may be required. Finding the right course can be a challenge.

Poor sleeping patterns are generally a symptom of something else going on within the person so the underlying cause needs to be determined. It might be a learned pattern from childhood or the result of a stressor or illness.

A 'natural therapy' approach is often an eclectic one that encompasses any number of healing modalities to suit the temperament and specific needs of the individual.

The natural therapist examines the person as a whole being; they do not separate a sore limb, upset tummy or bronchial infection from what is going on in the rest of the body, mind and life.

Taking a holistic approach to your health will mean that you need to make different commitments to yourself and your family. Lifestyle change is often necessary in order to bring healing. Changes may be simple or profound, including factors such as diet, relationships and the environment you live and work in.

This book provides many alternatives and guidelines to assist you to find your sleep solution. However, we do not recommend self medication. Herbal formulas sold in pharmacies, health food shops or on internet sites are generally harmless, however, they may have detrimental effects.

People who are on medication for conditions such as high blood pressure or depression, have a major kidney or heart complaint, or disorders such as epilepsy and diabetes, are pregnant, lactating or have allergic tendencies, should consult a health specialist before taking anything.

Also, natural does not equal harmless in all cases. Herbs are medicines and any substance that has a therapeutic action has the potential to interact with other medications and cause problematic side effects if taken by the wrong person or in the wrong dose.

Self medication may be appropriate in certain circumstances such as using herbs like Echinacea for colds or hay fever. However, horse radish and garlic capsules can have the effect of thinning the blood and are dangerous if taken 2-3 weeks before surgery as they can induce bleeding.

Seeing a qualified and experienced natural therapist or integrative medicine doctor is the most efficient and effective way to find a solution. This is because they will take a detailed history including your state of health and emotions as well as lifestyle so that they can construct a formula that will specifically suit your constitution and symptoms; but more about that later.

The function of sleep is to cure sleepiness.

– Old joke

CHAPTER 8

Sleep Quiz

The following questionnaire has been devised to help you determine whether you have a sleep disorder.

If your answer is yes to five or more of the following questions, and you experience these symptoms regularly, i.e. three times a week or more, then it is possible that you have a sleep disorder and it is time to contact your favourite health professional for advice before things get out of hand.

Table 8.1

Sl. No	Symptoms	Yes/No
1.	Do you sleep less than 5 hours a night?	
2.	Do you fall asleep as soon as your head hits the pillow?	

3.	Are you sleeping for more than 9 hours?	
4.	Do you work night shift?	
5.	Do you eat dinner late at night?	
6.	Are you exercising close to bedtime?	
7.	Are you experiencing anxiety or depression?	
8.	Do you experience difficulty sleeping before menstruation?	
9.	Is regular travel and crossing more than one time zone, part of your work/lifestyle?	
10.	Do you consume caffeine and or alcohol before bedtime?	
11.	Are you eating chocolate before going to bed?	
12.	Do you eat anything sweet before bedtime?	
13.	Do you take recreational drugs?	
14.	Are your meal times irregular?	
15.	Do the times you go to sleep and wake up, vary often?	
16.	Are you having difficulty switching your brain off at night?	
17.	Do you watch television in bed?	
18.	Do you have difficulty relaxing your legs while in bed?	
19.	Are your legs aching?	
20.	Do you experience neck, lower back or joint pain at night?	
21.	Is your mind lacking its usual sharpness? That is, are you experiencing mental dullness?	
22.	Is your recent memory impaired?	
23.	Do you suffer from tension, fear and anxiety?	
24.	Are you having regular headaches?	

Sleep Quiz

25.	Do you have a tendency to be bored or depressed?	
26.	Are you finding it difficult to be cooperative or are you unable to accept constructive criticism?	
27.	Are you irritable and prone to outbursts of temper?	
28.	Is your attention span shorter?	
29.	Has interest in your personal care lessened?	
30.	Do you or your partner snore?	
31.	Do you or your partner have restless legs in bed?	
32.	Has your sex drive decreased?	
33.	Are you waking up at night and unable to fall back to sleep within 20 minutes?	
34.	Do you wake up during the night to go to the bathroom?	
35.	Do you eat during the night?	
36.	Do you sleep walk?	
37.	Do you sleep talk?	
38.	Do you have nightmares?	
39.	Do you suffer from sleep apnoea?	
40.	Are you taking any kind of medication?	
41.	Are you aware of having any food allergies?	
42.	Do you have a serious or chronic illness?	
43.	Do you nap during the day?	
44.	Do you experience sleepiness during the day?	
45.	Is there electronic equipment on in your bedroom while you sleep such as a television or computer?	

How did you go? If you did not rate all that well then read on and rest assured that you can relearn the ancient act of sleeping. Understanding how and why sleep disorders occur will help you to work towards empowering yourself to make changes in your life.

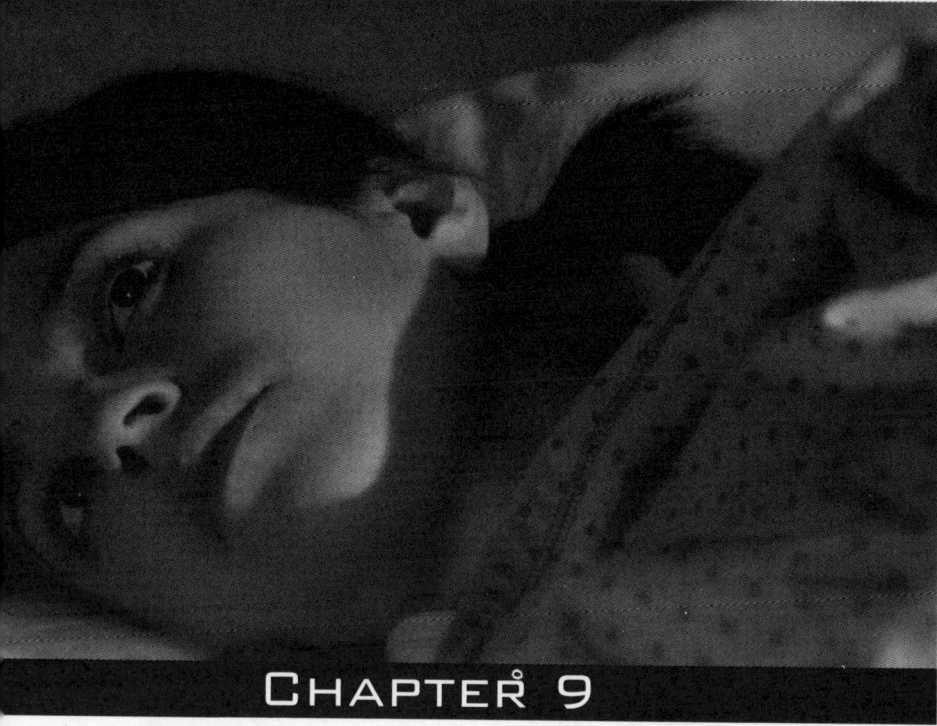

CHAPTER 9

The Many Ways in which We Cannot Sleep

Sleep disturbances take several forms:
- ✦ Insomnia or inability to sleep
- ✦ Waking up throughout the night
- ✦ Vivid dreams
- ✦ Bad dreams and night terrors
- ✦ Snoring
- ✦ Bed wetting
- ✦ Apnoeas

These disturbances cause us to wake up feeling unrefreshed, only to drag ourselves through a day, where we at worse struggle to stay awake and at best feel tired most of the time.

Specific Disorders in-depth

Sleep Apnoea

Apnoea means an intermittent cessation of breathing during sleep. Sleep apnoea is a common and serious condition.

When we fall asleep, our muscles tend to relax and become floppy. This includes the muscles in the back of the throat. While we sleep the muscles of the soft palate, and a piece of soft tissue in the back of the throat called the uvula, tend to relax and vibrate when the person breathes.

It matters not whether we breathe through the nose or mouth, this relaxed and floppy tissue vibrates as the air moves back and forth across it causing us to make that annoying snoring noise.

In some people the muscles become so floppy that they completely collapse. This obstructs breathing. The collapse is brief, usually for around 10 seconds, and it forces the person to repeatedly wake up to take breaths of air.

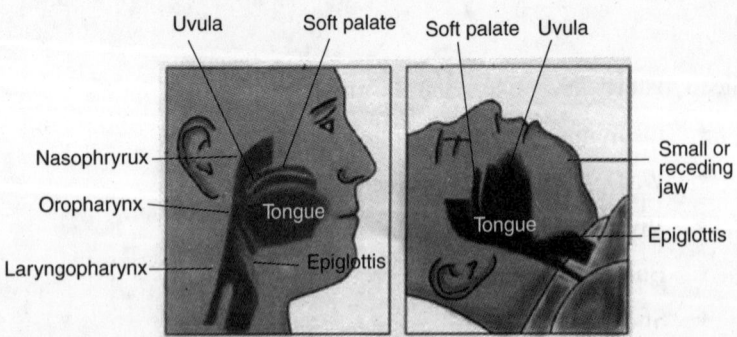

Fig. 9.1 *Anatomy of the throat and mouth. Sleep apnoea is caused by the muscles of the back of the throat and tongue collapsing during sleep and blocking the airways.*

In extreme cases, a person may stop breathing hundreds of times a night for as long as a minute. Arousal from sleep may only last a few seconds so it is not remembered in the morning, however the consequences will be the same the next day, that is, feeling excessively tired (Fig. 9.1).

Breathless in Bed

There are two types of sleep apnoea – obstructive sleep apnoea (OSA) and the less common central sleep apnoea (CSA). Central sleep apnoea is less common and occurs when the brain fails to signal the muscles that control breathing. Complex sleep apnoea is a combination of both types. The severity of the condition depends on how often the breathing is interrupted.

Diagnosis may be difficult without someone paying close attention to what is occurring while you sleep so you may need to attend a sleep clinic and have a 'polysomnograph' or sleep study.

People with sleep apnoea commonly display the following characteristics:

+ Apnoeas of between 10 seconds and 2 minutes or more
+ Snoring
+ Restlessness, excessive movement or kicking while asleep (restless legs)
+ Breathing through the mouth
+ Have a dry mouth and/or throat on waking
+ Being thirsty during the night and/or on waking
+ Waking feeling unrefreshed, daytime tiredness and an inability to think clearly
+ Tendency to fall asleep in meetings or in front of the television
+ Breathlessness when exercising

Sleep Apnoea and Your Body Clock

Your body schedule, which is governed by the circadian rhythm, is thrown out of kilter by the effects of interrupted breathing.

For example at night, the bronchi – small airways in the lungs – become narrow. They are dilated only enough to accommodate the relatively minimal needs of a resting body. However, because they are minimally dilated they are also more sensitive to broncho-constriction (narrowing of the airways). This is an additional problem for asthmatics who are sensitive to allergens such as the dust mites that abound in beds.

These allergens provoke a typical allergic reaction in the already constricted bronchi and the result is a disproportionate incidence of asthma compared with daytime. The problem is even more serious for asthmatics who suffer from sleep apnoea.

A combination of an interrupted circadian rhythm, plus changes in the airways during sleep, and changes to the airways triggered by environmental allergens such as dust and mites, can cause serious illness.

High Alert

You may have heard stories about people gaining enough strength in an emergency to lift a car off an accident victim. This is the sympathetic nervous system in action. The sympathetic nervous system rallies when a person is in a state of perceived threat and it activates the flight or fight response.

In these situations, blood pressure increases and the heart beats faster. During sleep apnoea the person stops breathing so the brain perceives this as an emergency and activates the sympathetic nervous system, placing the body on high alert.

This is not an ideal stress to have your body experience each night when it is meant to be resting and repairing.

Apnoea Symptoms According to the Time of Day

Table 9.1

Daytime symptoms	Night time symptoms
Excessive Daytime Sleepiness (EDS)	Loud snoring, choking
	Breathing stops
Taking naps that are not refreshing	Sitting up, fighting for sleep
Personality change	
Morning headaches	Abnormal motor movements
Inability to concentrate	Oesophageal reflux
Impotence	Frequent urination
Profuse sweating	

Link between Apnoea and Other Conditions

People who suffer from sleep apnoea have an increased risk of cardiovascular complications and the condition is associated with premature ill health and disability. A number of serious illnesses are connected with sleep apnoea.

Diabetes

A high proportion of people with type 2 diabetes also suffer from sleep apnoea. However, the links between the two conditions need to be further investigated.

Where it can get tricky is that people suffering from diabetes are often tired so a person who also has sleep apnoea could go undiagnosed.

Having a Hypo

Hypoglycaemia is a metabolic condition that causes the blood glucose level to drop. When this happens at night (nocturnal hypoglycaemia) it can cause insomnia. This is common for people with type 1 diabetes.

Depending on the severity, a person may be either asymptomatic (symptom-free), or have symptoms such as night sweats, restiveness and nightmares or in even more severe conditions, it can cause convulsions, and coma or even death.

Excessive consumption of refined carbohydrates (includes white rice and pasta) is one of the main culprits exacerbating hypoglycaemia and diabetes. Having a better diet will influence the severity of the disorder.

A drop in blood glucose level causes the release of hormones that regulate glucose levels. These compounds stimulate the brain and signal that it is time to eat.

Bedtime snacks that help keep blood sugar levels regular throughout the night are whole grain cereals such as oatmeal, whole grain breads and other complex carbohydrates. These foods also promote sleep by increasing serotonin levels.

Hypopnoea

Hypopnoea is a condition similar to apnoea. However, breathing only stops partially here. It is usually defined as a 50 per cent decrease in breathing as compared to breathing when awake.

As with apnoea, the muscles collapse in the back of the throat stopping the progress of air. However with hypopnoea, breathing stops from a fraction of a second for up to 30 or 40 seconds or more.

Treatment for Sleep Apnoea

A treatment preferred by doctors for people with moderate to serious obstructive sleep apnoea is the nocturnal use of a continuous positive airway pressure (CPAP) machine.

A mask fits over the nose and/or mouth and is attached to a CPAP machine. The machine increases air pressure in the throat stopping the airway from collapsing on the inward breath.

Research shows that CPAP is effective because it stops the apnoea thus decreasing daytime sleepiness, especially in those with moderate to severe sleep apnoea. However, it may not be as effective for people who have mild sleep apnoea.

Studies also show that it can lower blood pressure, day and night, so people with coronary artery disease who use CPAP for sleep apnoea are less likely to have heart problems such as heart failure.

It can take time to become comfortable with using CPAP. If you cannot get used to it, talk to your doctor. You might be able to try another type of mask or make other adjustments.

There are some risks. It can cause nightmares and excessive dreaming during early use as well as nosebleeds, sore throat, nasal congestion and headaches. Rare complications are bacterial infection in the lining around the brain and spinal cord (meningitis), and severe nosebleeds.

Oral appliances such as dental appliances and mouthpieces are used to treat teeth grinding and temporomandibular joint (TMJ) problems. They are also useful for treatment of snoring and in some cases, mild to moderate sleep apnoea.

Another very effective modality for the treatment of sleep apnoea is the Buteyko breathing method (see page 223).

Gastroesophageal Reflux Disorder (GERD)

This condition results from stomach acid backing up into the throat during the night (acid reflux). The acid irritates and inflames the tissues that are involved in sleep apnoea episodes.

There is contention over whether apnoea triggers reflux or whether it is the other way around. Some researchers believe that apnoea leads to changes in airway pressure causing reflux to occur. Other researchers think that the reflux of acids causes spasms of the tissues around the vocal cords and subsequently triggers apnoea. Either way it is a problem to be solved.

Bedtime can be burn time if a person is sensitive to spicy and acidic foods. Heartburn will surely prevent sleep, which is an added problem for people suffering from GERD. Lying down makes heartburn worse, and the discomfort from heartburn hinders sleep.

Snoring

Snoring in the Land Down Under

Studies conducted among the general population in the Hunter Valley, a beautiful wine producing region in Australia's New South Wales, suggest that at least one in every 25 people (4 per cent) have sleep apnoea. Similar results have been found in other studies across the world.

Those who do not live alone may not relish that stunning symphony of wind against soft palate that occurs while someone near and dear sleeps. This is otherwise known as snoring.

If your partner snores, it might be some small comfort to know that you are not alone; it is very common. Snoring is a sleep condition and so is living with a snorer because this person is also prevented from sleeping.

Women are more likely than men to complain about their bed partner snoring because men are more likely to snore. There is no clear reason for this. Approximately 40 per cent of men snore. However ladies, if you think you are immune, think again because around 24 per cent of you do it regularly and even babies snore sometimes when they have a cold.

Snoring occurs mostly during sleep and there are some serious risks associated with it:

+ There is the risk to relationships; share a bed with a snorer and say goodnight to sleep. Two grumpy, sleep deprived people do not make for a good relationship
+ Snorers are prone to develop problems with their heart and blood pressure and have an increased risk of stroke. In fact, studies show that a loud snorer has a higher risk of stroke and heart disease compared to those who do not snore

A research study called 'Cardiovascular Disease and Healthcare Utilization in Snorers: A Population Survey' was reported in the journal *Sleep*. Hungarian scientists studied 12,643 snorers. The group represented 0.16 per cent of the Hungarian population over the age of 18 years across the country.

Results showed that people who snored loudly had a 40 per cent greater chance of having hypertension, a 34 per cent increased chance of having a heart attack and were 67 per cent more likely to have a stroke compared with those who do not snore.

Female snorers who snored quietly had an increased risk of hypertension.

Loud snoring was also associated with increased use of health care resources such as being hospitalised.

Another study found that heavy snorers are six times more likely to suffer a heart attack while asleep. This is because the risk of heart disease can be increased due to blood pressure, and nerve and hormonal changes caused by snoring. People who suffer from obstructive sleep apnoea are most at risk.

It is also speculated that breathing interruptions decrease the oxygen flow to the brain, which increases the risk of having a stroke.

The British Snoring and Sleep Association advise that anyone who snores should get treated immediately. Sounds like a sensible course of action.

Restless Leg Syndrome (RLS)

If your legs seem to have a mind of their own when you lie down to sleep, then you have restless legs syndrome (RLS). If you have RLS you have an overwhelming need to move your legs. Approximately one in ten people have this condition.

RLS is a neurological disorder. Symptoms range in severity from the merely uncomfortable to severe and excruciating. The uncontrollable urge to move is at its peak when sitting or lying still. In fact, the very act of relaxing and resting sets the symptoms in motion. The longer people with RLS remain still, the worse their symptoms become.

RLS does not only occur during sleep. You might occasionally see people in public places who are unable to sit still. They continually move their feet, shift their weight or scratch. They may or may not be conscious of their movements.

However, as annoying as RLS can be when people are fully awake, when it happens during sleep it becomes a much more serious problem. Generally, symptoms are worse in the evening, and they are aggravated further by lying down.

Research has shown that people who suffer from RLS also suffer disproportionately from anxiety, depression and nervous tension. This is not hard to imagine because it would be a very aggravating condition.

Also, 80 per cent of people who suffer from RLS also have periodic limb movement disorder (PLMD). This means their legs move in jerks and twitches at 20-30 second intervals repeatedly throughout the night, which often wakes them. Imagine sharing a bed with someone who poked and kicked your legs hard enough to wake you up 2-3 times a minute all night.

Sensations experienced through both these conditions vary in severity and are generally experienced on both sides of the body lasting for a few minutes or an hour. They can be felt deep inside the leg from the knee to the ankle and sometimes in the hands, thighs, feet and arms.

Skin sensations include:
- Itching
- Tingling
- Creeping or crawling
- Burning, searing
- Tugging
- Aching
- Alternating feelings of heat and cold
- Electric current like sensations in the legs

The condition is a mysterious one because there is generally no known cause. It can occur at any age. However, people may be more likely to suffer from it in middle or old age or during pregnancy.

PLMD can also be hereditary (50 per cent of cases being inherited) and a side effect of certain medications such as antidepressants. It can also be caused by iron deficiency. People who have narcolepsy and Parkinson's disease may also have these symptoms, and it is also more common in insomniacs. In fact, it exacerbates insomnia because it can prevent the person from going back to sleep.

In a hopeless bid to divest themselves of the sensations, the sufferer squirms and wriggles in bed, or gets up and paces about. Stretching the legs sometimes helps, as does resting the legs on a cold surface. However, on returning to bed the sensations start again.

Fortunately, in most people symptoms are mild and can be fairly well controlled. As the condition is basically a sleep disorder, taking steps to get a good night's sleep will often provide relief in less severe cases.

For partners of those who have this disorder, it might be a good idea to sleep in a separate bed until the condition is under control.

How to Determine Whether You Have Restless Leg Syndrome

If you have any of the following symptoms or irresistible urges then you may have RLS. If you suspect this, consult your health practitioner.

Table 9.2

Sl. No	Symptoms	Yes/No
1.	Are you unable to resist the urge to move your legs when you are sitting or lying down?	
2.	Do you feel an unpleasant, creepy-crawly sensation deep inside your legs?	
3.	Do these sensations occur during periods of rest or inactivity and are they worse during periods of relaxation?	
4.	Are these symptoms reduced or relieved by voluntary leg movements?	

5.	Do the feelings and movements happen more in the night, especially, when you lie down, than during the day?	
6.	Do you often have trouble falling asleep or staying asleep?	
7.	Is the jerking of your legs more evident after a stressful day?	
8.	Are you frequently tired or unable to concentrate during the day?	
9.	Do members of your family experience the same kind of unpleasant sensations and urges to move?	
10.	Have medical tests failed to reveal a cause for the uncontrollable urge to move and the unpleasant sensations?	

Bed is a Tango Free Zone

Use some common sense and listen to your body when working out how to manage this condition. If you are having difficulty falling and staying asleep there are a number of basic things you can do such as use herbal medicines (see page 175) and lifestyle modifications. RLS can also be exacerbated by a lack of certain minerals.

Treatment

When legs seem to want to dance the following treatments can help:

- ✦ Walking or stretching exercises will help circulation (poor circulation has been associated with RLS)
- ✦ Hot or cold baths
- ✦ Massaging the legs
- ✦ Heat or cold packs on the legs

- Minerals such as magnesium and calcium as well as wide spectrum colloidal minerals and iron are very useful for RLS

Good sleep hygiene and getting plenty of sleep will also assist restless legs because being tired can make the symptoms worse.

Smoking and drinking caffeine and alcohol can also aggravate the condition. Studies have shown that RLS is more common among smokers. Stopping smoking and reducing or avoiding stimulants like alcohol and caffeine will help reduce symptoms and improve general health.

The movements can also increase due to stress. Find ways that suit you to manage stress. There are so many ways to do this such as yoga, meditation or taking a bath. Engage in activities that you enjoy, such as gardening, painting or reading, that transport you into a happier more contented space.

However, if symptoms are severe and they do not respond to these measures, the next step may be medication. Simple analgesics such as aspirin or paracetamol may help. If not, a doctor may prescribe a drug called a dopamine agonist.

Some of the medications can have side effects so make sure you are well informed about them. Ideally, drugs should be used during periods when the symptoms are particularly troubling and stopped when symptoms cease.

Herbs for RLS

Following are a number of herbs and minerals that are useful in treating RLS. These will need to be prescribed by a qualified herbalist.

- Astragalus balances and improves the function of the organs by increasing blood circulation, improving iron absorption and boosting immunity

- Butcher's broom helps circulation and relieves discomfort and pain
- Horse chestnut enhances circulation of the blood
- Zinc used for RLS assists absorption of minerals such as iron and it has a calming effect
- Magnesium phosphate maintains the body's level of magnesium. Lack of magnesium can cause muscle spasms

Narcolepsy

If someone suddenly drops off to sleep while talking to you, do not worry, it is probably not a comment on your personality; it might just be that they are suffering from narcolepsy.

This is a chronic neurological disorder that affects one in 2000 people. It is caused by the brain's inability to regulate the sleep-wake cycles normally.

People who suffer from narcolepsy have momentary urges to fall asleep throughout the day. If that urge overwhelms them they will actually fall asleep for periods that last from a few to several minutes. In rare cases people sleep for an hour or longer.

Symptoms Associated with Narcolepsy

- Excessive daytime sleepiness (EDS) with a tendency to fall asleep without warning. This at worst is dangerous, especially, if the person is driving a car, and at least disconcerting having, negative effects on lifestyle
- Cataplexy, which is a sudden loss of voluntary muscle control, can be triggered by intense emotions such as anger or surprise or during laughter. A cataplectic attack lasts from a few seconds up to 30 minutes and causes:
  - Facial muscles to sag
  - The head to nod

- Knees to buckle
- Loss of strength in the arms
- Garbled speech
- Immediate collapse of the body

✦ Vivid dreams like hallucinations during the onset of sleep or while waking up. This can be very frightening as the person is often partially awake

✦ Brief episodes of total paralysis occur at the beginning or end of sleep where the person cannot move or speak

✦ Automatic behaviour, which involves performing routine tasks while sleeping. On waking there is no memory of what has taken place – this is also a potentially dangerous situation

✦ Difficulty staying asleep at night, which makes the person more tired during the day

✦ Reduced quality of life due to excessive sleepiness, plus sleep attacks are generally misunderstood and considered socially unacceptable. This lack of understanding can detrimentally impact a person's self-esteem, strain personal relationships and lead to psychological problems

✦ Being excessively tired during the day affects a person's ability to work, concentrate and remember. It can also lead to erratic moods and depression. That is why it is crucial to identify narcolepsy in children at the earliest possible age, in order to avoid developing low self-esteem and a lifetime pattern of failure

The cause of narcolepsy is not known and there is no cure, however, the condition can be managed. Often it begins in the teenage years but it can be hard to diagnose because symptoms can appear progressively and falling asleep in a classroom could be attributed to other factors such as too many late nights or disinterest in the activities.

Treatment Options

A combination treatment of pharmaceutical drugs prescribed by a sleep specialist will provide stimulation to improve alertness and anti-depressants to control cataplexy, sleep induced hallucinations and sleep paralysis.

These medications can have side effects and it is a matter of finding a suitable balance between symptom control and side effects.

If your condition warrants medication then it may be helpful to supplement these with lifestyle and behavioural strategies. For example, many people with narcolepsy take short, regularly scheduled naps at times when they are feeling sleepiest.

People with narcolepsy can enhance general sleep quality through maintaining a regular sleep schedule and practicing good sleep habits such as avoiding alcohol and caffeine before bedtime. By improving the quality of night time sleep, excessive sleepiness during the day is reduced, which will help relieve the constant fatigue.

Diagnosis

If you think you might have symptoms of narcolepsy then see a sleep specialist. If narcolepsy is suspected, you may be required to undergo a number of tests at a sleep centre to confirm the diagnosis and the severity.

CHAPTER 10

Why Many Women Find it Hard to Sleep

The person who says it cannot be done should not interrupt the person doing it.

– Chinese proverb

Those special hormones that relate to the functioning of the female reproduction system, progesterone and oestrogen, are known in some cases to govern the lives of women who suffer from a lack of their equilibrium.

Biological factors unique to women like menstruation, pregnancy and menopause, affect sleep quality because of fluctuating hormone levels that happen over the course of a month and indeed a lifetime.

And, if you consider all the side effects that come about due to hormonal imbalances at various stages in a woman's lifetime, menses to menopause, then life has the potential to be fairly challenging.

Following is a list of symptoms that can occur if a woman's hormones are not in balance:

- Bloating around the abdomen
- Breast swelling and tenderness
- Headaches ranging from mild to a severe migraine
- Tiredness, lethargy and insomnia
- Weight gain
- Constipation
- Food cravings, especially sweet foods
- Aches and pains, particularly lower back, legs and abdomen
- Poor coordination or clumsiness
- Skin problems such as acne
- Short, intense energy boosts
- Irritability
- Anxiety
- Nervous tension
- Mood swings
- Lower coping ability
- Depression
- Aggression
- Difficulty concentrating
- Lower libido or, rarely, increased libido
- Feeling unloved
- Wanting to be alone
- Reduced interest in work and social life

Go with the Flow

Sleep and the Menstruation Cycle
Anita had that Cramping Feeling

> *Anita bemoaned the fact she was seemingly premenstrual for most of the month.*
>
> *First there were the ovulation pains that sometimes had the intensity of appendicitis.*
>
> *Then she was beset by PMS symptoms making her moody, snappy with her family and prone to feeling depressed. She craved cake and chocolates, and lay awake at night.*
>
> *When her period finally arrived there were the migraines, excruciating cramps, a bearing down feeling in her thighs, sleepless nights pondering her stomach pains, and, well, need we go on?*

***

If like Anita, your hormones are out of balance for any reason, be it lifestyle factors, poor nutrition or stress, then this may affect your periods. Many women do suffer from the following list of symptoms prior to menstruating each month for their whole menstruating life:

- Mood swings
- Irregular menstrual cycle
- Loss of mental clarity and focus
- Depression
- Sore breasts
- Fluid retention/bloating
- Loss of libido
- Fibroid cysts in the uterus
- Breast lumps

- Carbohydrate cravings (sweets, cakes, chocolates, and pastries
- Emotional outburst (crying, anger, frustration)
- Migraines
- Insomnia

A poll conducted by the National Sleep Foundation (USA) revealed that half of all menstruating women surveyed reported that bloating disturbed their sleep for 2-3 days during the period. These changes can be linked to the rise and fall of hormone levels in the body.

The first few days of menstrual bleeding are the least restful and 36 per cent of women report having unsatisfying sleep while menstruating. This translates into an average of 60 hours of disturbed sleep per month. Insomnia and excessive sleepiness or hypersomnia are common effects of PMS.

During the period of life when a woman menstruates, she also ovulates in the middle of each cycle. In the days following ovulation, women may find it difficult to fall asleep because of declining levels of progesterone. Conversely, elevated levels of progesterone early in pregnancy seem to be linked with a strong tendency to sleep.

This is a message to women and the men who live with them; this is not a hopeless cause! These issues can be addressed in a number of ways including diet, lifestyle and natural medicines.

Moody Blues – Premenstrual Dysphoric Disorder (PMDD)

PMS refers to the physical and mood symptoms that appear during the last 1-2 weeks of the menstrual cycle and disappear by the end of the menses. Women with PMS may also have an underlying circadian disturbance or disruption that causes them to either wake too early in the morning or sleep too late.

PMDD describes a specific set of mood symptoms that are also present the week before the menses. These symptoms include depressed moods, emotional volatility, irritability, decreased interest in usual activities, difficulty in concentrating, lack of energy, a marked change in appetite, overeating or food cravings, feelings of being overwhelmed and sleepiness or insomnia.

Around 75-85 per cent of women have cyclic menses symptoms.

Keeping a diary is a useful tool to help diagnose whether you have PMS or PMDD, and sleep disorders. Noting daily symptoms and correlating them with general sleep patterns is valuable for diagnosis.

The diary helps you see a pattern of daytime symptoms and makes the connection to the associated sleep disturbances more obvious. Trying to remember all the symptoms and when they occurred can be difficult, especially if you are recalling them weeks later to a health professional.

Understanding your body and its symptoms will enable you to work with a health practitioner to determine the most effective treatment to return the natural balance to your body to achieve trouble free female functions.

Treatment of Menstruation-related Sleep Disorders

Generally, menstrual-related insomnia disappears a few days after the period is finished. However, the following tips will help sleep difficulties during menstruation:

- ✦ Maintain a regular sleep/wake schedule
- ✦ Avoid stress where possible

- Take regular exercise
- Practice good sleep hygiene

Dietary Changes for a Happy Period

- Eat a low carbohydrate diet, especially avoiding simple sugars as sugar will feed the tummy cramps
- Reduce or eliminate caffeine
- Calcium supplements have been shown to reduce symptoms in some women
- Evening primrose oil

Pregnancy

Being pregnant is a wonderful experience for most women. However, for many it can also be a time when sleeping becomes a big challenge, regardless of how sound sleep was prior to pregnancy.

According to the National Sleep Foundation's (USA) 1998 'Women and Sleep' poll, 78 per cent of women report more disturbed sleep during pregnancy than at other times.

Poor sleep can lead to a number of problems in expectant mothers such as an increased likelihood of becoming depressed as well as causing attention and memory problems. And of course all this will result in excessive daytime sleepiness.

It is hardly surprising then that many pregnant women are tired.

Sleep Patterns During Pregnancy

Changes in hormone levels at various stages of pregnancy as well as levels of discomfort that occur as the baby grows, affects the sleep patterns of a mother to be. In the third trimester, approximately, 75 per cent of women have disrupted sleep.

Physical discomfort is felt due to the increasing size of the baby, and there may be a whole host of related symptoms such as heartburn, leg cramps, pressure on the bladder and even congested sinuses that interrupt sleep.

Lifestyle factors can also affect stress levels and sleep. Many women continue working until they are close to the time of giving birth so they are juggling the pressures of work, home and other children.

The American Academy of Sleep Medicine recommends that one of the ways for expectant mothers to give their baby a better chance of a healthy, full term birth is through practicing good sleep hygiene.

RLS Wriggles into Pregnancy

It is more common for women to develop restless leg syndrome in the third trimester; between 15-25 per cent of pregnant women develop this condition. Hormone fluctuations are partially responsible as well as iron deficiency and low folate levels. These deficiencies can be addressed through supplementation, however, make sure you consult with your health professional who will give a proper diagnosis and prescription.

RLS generally ceases after giving birth, however it is another sleep disrupter that will make a woman weary.

Pregnancy and Apnoea

Developing sleep apnoea is a high risk factor for pregnant women who are obese and those who gain excessive weight during pregnancy. This is potentially dangerous because a drop in blood oxygen levels at night is associated with potential complications for the baby. A woman who is overweight or gains a lot of weight during pregnancy should be assessed by a doctor in case sleep apnoea has developed.

Snoring in Pregnancy

So much change happens to a woman's body while she is growing a baby. She may never have uttered a gentle night time sonorant squeak from the back of her palate but during pregnancy she may snore like an oncoming freight train. This is because hormone changes can cause the nasal passages to swell, producing non-allergic rhinitis and blocked airways.

Just because it is due to pregnancy, and the mother is a first time snorer, does not mean the snoring should be neglected. If it is apnoea, the reduced oxygen supply affects both the mother and the baby. Also, snoring can lead to changes in the airway tissues that can make the mother inclined to snore or experience apnoea after the baby is born.

Sleep disordered breathing and snoring can:

- Increase the incidence of pre-eclampsia two-fold
- Increase the rate of hypertension
- Result in a smaller foetus

This has led some doctors and health care providers to carefully screen for snoring and sleep apnoea in patients who are at high risk of pre-eclampsia. Screening tests may include urine and blood tests as well as a sleep study. Snoring mothers to be should definitely seek professional advice.

Pregnancy and Night Shift

A double whammy for mummy and tummy is when a pregnant women works night shift. Disruptions to the circadian clock can cause a whole other host of problems.

A Danish study published in the American Journal of Obstetrics and Gynecology shows that working night shift increases the risk of delivering a child that is past the due date by 35 per cent.

Also women working night shift have an increased risk of between 50-80 per cent of having babies with low birth weight.

According to the researchers, night work may prolong the duration of pregnancy and reduce foetal growth, especially among industrial workers. Industrial workers with fixed night work had a high risk of post-term birth.

Looking After Yourself During Pregnancy

One of the most important life activities is growing a baby. For this, a woman deserves and needs to take care of and even pamper herself.

Here are some great ways to increase chances of a good sleep while pregnant:

- Have a warm bath just before bed and ask your partner to massage your back, shoulders and neck to help you relax
- During the second and third trimester sleep on your left side. This will enhance the blood flow to the uterus, kidneys and foetus. Do not lie on your back for any more than a brief period
- Be sensible and listen to your body. If you have heartburn, avoid spicy and acidic foods
- Sleep with your upper body raised 6-8 inches and avoid lying down for two hours after eating
- If you are prone to nausea, eat small snacks of bland food, drink chamomile or ginger tea and keep your stomach full. Lining the stomach can help relieve that sick feeling
- Take cat naps
- Watch funny films
- Meditate

As mentioned earlier, some pregnant women develop restless leg syndrome. If you begin to have some of those symptoms such as creeping or crawling feelings in your legs on lying down then try some leg stretches, take a walk or massage your legs, and inform your health practitioner.

Post-partum Slumber

Traditionally, mothers and fathers alike can expect to forget about the 's' word (sleep) for some time after giving birth. So parents, if you possibly can, make sure you have a good support system in place to give mum a regular break for a good night's sleep.

A breast pump means that feeding time can be a shared experience. And it is empowering for fathers to bond with the baby in this way.

It is believed that a major contributor to post-partum depression is sleep deprivation. At the first sign of the blues talk to your family, friends and health practitioner.

Tips for Lactating Mothers

Mum, if your baby is having difficulty settling, examine your diet. Onions, garlic, some spices and stimulants such as coffee will transfer to the baby and stimulate them so it is best to avoid these foods.

Drinking chamomile tea will calm you and the baby. Relaxing exercises and breathing techniques are also useful before bed.

Remember, the more relaxed and rested you are, the more relaxed your baby will be.

Change of Life

Peri-menopause generally begins when a woman reaches her late forties and early fifties, and in increasing cases, women in their late thirties are experiencing this change. Many changes are associated with this time of life alongside hormonal ones.

It is well termed the 'change of life' because it is often a time of change on the physical and emotional levels. This is because:

- A woman at this time of life needs to come to terms with entering a new period where she is aging and no longer fertile
- It is likely that her children are in the process of leaving or have left home
- She may have retired from work
- It is a common time for marriages to breakup
- There are serious hormonal changes and fluctuations occurring

All these stressors can contribute to insomnia and chronic sleep deprivation as well as mood and behavioural fluctuations.

Changes in hormonal activity during menopause cause not only the cessation of the menstrual cycle but a host of other symptoms, which vary according to the amount of stress in the individual's life, the state of the woman's health and hormone levels.

- A study published in the journal, *Sleep and Breathing* (2003), found that reductions in female sex hormones (specifically progesterone and oestradiol, the primary oestrogen) were associated with an increased probability of sleep disordered breathing

The following list of symptoms can manifest with menopause:

- Migraine
- Depression
- Loss of libido
- Fibroid cysts in the uterus
- Breast lumps
- Loss of skin tone and development of jowls
- Mood swings
- Irregular menstrual cycle
- Loss of mental clarity and focus
- Dry vagina
- Infertility
- Weight gain
- Hot flushes
- Obesity
- Insulin resistance
- Low blood sugar
- Emotional outburst (crying, anger, frustration)
- Loss of bone density
- Restless leg syndrome
- Sleep disorders

Menopause and Sleeplessness

Sleep disruption is a common symptom of menopause where there is hormonal imbalance.

Progesterone raises body temperature and helps induce sleep. Researchers have linked low levels of progesterone, usually a result of peri-menopause and menopause, with a longer time period between stage 1 sleep and REM sleep. This means less time is spent in the deep restful stage of sleep.

Importantly, oestrogen deficiency can cause a deficit of brain neurotransmitters such as serotonin, which can trigger insomnia.

Sleeping off Menopause

> *Researchers kept track of a group of menopausal women with chronic sleep problems after giving them oestradiol supplements. They found that over 70 per cent of the women reported sleeping well after treatment. And all the women noticed an improvement in symptoms such as hot flushes and night sweats, which often disrupt sleep during peri-menopause and menopause.*

Emotional and physiological changes that happen throughout menopause often affect sleep patterns as well as increasing stress levels and causing fatigue, exhaustion and possibly depression. And of course restful sleep is vital to combating all of these problems so there lays another difficulty.

Snoring can become severe for peri-menopausal women. This can come about because of changes in body fat distribution affecting the shape of the upper airway.

The increase in abdominal girth during menopause may explain why sleep apnoea increases 3-4 times in menopausal women. A decrease in progesterone is also suspected as a cause for the increased incidence. This problem seems to be exacerbated with age as 1 in 4 women over the age of 65 experience sleep apnoea.

Because it is well-known that apnoea is associated with hypertension, stroke and heart disease, it is best not to leave the condition untreated.

Awake in a Flash

Given the fluctuations of mood, behaviour and sleep that results from the hormonal roller coaster of menstruation, it is only logical that the decline of those hormonal cycles should result in some swings of their own.

Again, if hormones are out of balance, a woman may experience:

- Lower levels of oestrogen, which affect the hypothalamus. This part of the brain plays a principal role in regulating sleep cycles
- Decreased oestrogen levels send a false alarm to the brain that the body is too hot and so it reacts as it would to a high fever; the heart pumps faster and blood vessels in the skin dilate causing a woman to become hot and sweaty

This heat releasing mechanism is useful because it keeps the body temperature down when the weather is hot and when you exercise, but when there is a false alarm it results in hot flushes. Hot flushes last for about three minutes but the fun can go on for a year or several years. These 'hotties' also happen through the night making the perspiring, conscious woman throw the blankets off at regular intervals.

The experience of menopause can be difficult and challenging if a woman is not in optimum health. Find a good natural medicine practitioner to work with if you are peri-menopausal or menopausal. Some modalities are very effective in treating women's health issues including western herbalism and Chinese medicine.

CHAPTER 11

Getting Zapped – Electromagnetic Radiation (EMR) Affects Health and Sleep

Hidden forces can affect the quality of our sleep. We can clearly see the food we place in our mouths but we cannot observe our hormones. We can experience noise such as loud neighbour generated 'doof doof' music that keeps us awake at night, but we cannot see electromagnetic radiation.

The invisible force exists and they come from many sources – some good and some very bad.

Sources of Electromagnetic Radiation

- Planetary magnetic fields
- Electrical equipment such as quartz watches, high tension electric wires
- Electric blankets
- Water beds
- Movement of fluids such as storm water drains, water and gas pipes, underground rivers and streams
- Radioactivity including microwave ovens, radios, televisions and telephone transmission stations, visual display units, x-rays, air travel, security scanners and even jet lag is partly due to EMR
- Underground caves such as goldmines
- Halogen lights
- Magnets, such as those used for rheumatic and arthritic conditions

On a macro scale, the whole world is a massive magnet that generates electromagnetism. According to 'Dynamic theory', convection currents within the molten metal of the earth act like wires in a dynamo. All matter, including humans, is electric and magnetic. All our body's biochemical interactions are underpinned by electricity.

We can measure some of our electric currents with electroencephalograms and electrocardiograms (EEG and ECGs), which measure the currents in the brain and heart.

Sometimes, we experience static electric shock when we touch metal or walk on nylon carpet. These charges can reach up to 20,000-30,000 volts. Shocking!

Given that we naturally utilise electromagnetic activity for the normal functioning of our body and organs, it is not surprising that it can be interfered with by unseen forces that can deeply affect our well-being. One of these forces is geopathic stress caused by electromagnetic radiation.

Geopathic Stress

Geo means earth and pathos refers to disease.

A place where there is exposure to electromagnetic radiation (EMR) is called a geopathic zone. These zones have the potential to harm our immune, healing and repair systems.

Harmful EMR is emitted from particular locations and continued exposure will progressively wear down the healing and immune systems. In fact, these hidden forces are all around us most of the time and can cause disease in all beings; animals and humans, as well as psychological problems and insomnia.

Bedrooms are for Sleep not Electronic Entertainment

Electromagnetic fields (EMFs) can disrupt the pineal gland, which produces melatonin and serotonin, chemicals that are important for mood, sleep and other functions. EMFs are generated by electrical appliances like clocks, televisions and computers or geopathic stressors in the earth as well as electrical plants and phone towers.

Electronic devices are best kept out of the bedroom. This includes computers, clocks, mobile phones, phone chargers and televisions. If a device must be used, keep it as far away from the bed as possible, preferably at least three feet.

Halogen lights should not be used over beds as Electro Magnetic Radiation (EMR) is emitted from their transformers. If you do have to have halogen lights, maintain a distance of at least two metres from the transformers. It is best not to fit the transformers into the ceiling above the bed or desk.

Where you are situated in your bedroom's geography will have a huge impact on your health. This is because you are in bed for those eight hours generally without moving from that position; so if EMRs are constantly close to you for that time you are receiving a steady dose. The same applies if you have a desk in your bedroom and spend a lot of time at work or study.

Switch appliances in your bedroom off, or even unplug them before going to bed. Some people recommend disconnecting the circuit breaker prior to bed time to kill all the power in the house.

If you are suffering from a health condition, then engage an expert who can assess the electromagnetic fields (EMFs) in your home. You may be surprised at how common it is for people and pets to have health conditions that are exacerbated or caused by electromagnetic radiation.

Assessment of EMR Related Damage

A trained Feng Shui consultant or a building biologist can ascertain the health of a house and make recommendations regarding the placement of furniture such as beds and desks for study, as well as computers and televisions, so they are in positions that do not compromise health.

Feng Shui experts use different types of equipment to ascertain electromagnetic radiation such as a gauss metre, which measures EMR; a Geiger machine that measures underground activity such as ley lines and underground water; and a Luo pan, which is used to orient and evaluate north, south, east and west directions on a site.

An effective way to assess physical damage due to EMR is through diagnosis by electronic devices such as bioenergetic machines such as Vega or Mora machines. These conduct bio- energetic evaluation and measure the presence of geopathic stress on the body. These machines are so insightful, they can practically tell you what you had for breakfast, and more importantly, the type of geopathic stress that is causing the problems, even the fact that your bed may need to be moved.

If you are suffering from an unexplained illness or set of symptoms, or if there is a spate of cancer in the family, including your pets, it is worthwhile to cover all bases and get your house checked by a building biologist and/or Feng Shui specialist for EMF/EMR and other toxicities.

Building Biology-Sick Building Syndrome (SBS)

Nature is a bountiful entity. Left to itself it is a perfectly operating machine that creates everything we need for a healthy life.

It was only when people moved away from the natural rhythms of life and misused the bounty of the planet that they created the instruments that could potentially destroy us. One example is the materials we build our homes and workplaces from where we have manipulated and applied our natural resources in such a way that we are housed in a toxic environment.

Modern construction materials including carpets, laminates, floor finishes, adhesives and paints are made from toxic materials that can cause serious health issues. Some people are so sensitive that just by walking into a newly painted room they become dizzy, develop an instant headache and are unable to sleep. These are symptoms of 'sick building syndrome'.

The World Health Organisation (WHO) reports that a third of new buildings since 1960 are sick or toxic. Sick building syndrome costs Australians $12 billion a year. A sick building can cause sensitive dwellers serious symptoms ranging from fatigue, drowsiness, dizziness and headaches, to digestive and respiratory upsets and insomnia.

The effects of toxic building and construction materials linger long after the building is complete as materials emit gases into the air. This is known as 'off gassing'. The gases are most intense immediately after installation but they will continue to emit hazardous compounds over time. This toxicity is a problem in domestic environments and commercial and educational buildings.

To compound the problem, some countries such as Australia and Britain have a building regulation system where the building must be well sealed for greater energy efficiency. The idea that heat loss due to poorly sealed windows and doors is reduced, which is great from an energy efficiency point of view but it tends to create micro climates and effectively seals in fumes or toxic emissions within the home. This is emerging as a serious problem.

Reducing the Building Toxicity

If you are building a dwelling or commercial premises, consider the health of the occupants.

- ✦ Where possible natural materials should be employed. Ideally it is best to use natural fibres. Wool, natural oils, timber and stone are good alternatives to plastics and high gloss paints. There are also non-toxic paints on the market worth investigating
- ✦ Any new construction using materials such as adhesives, carpets, laminates, floor finishes and paint will off-gas into the air. These gases can cause serious health issues

- The gases are intense immediately after installation but they will certainly continue to emit hazardous compounds over time. By keeping fresh air circulating, toxicity will be reduced. So, ventilation is a key issue
- There is a shield available in the market to paint onto the interior walls that blocks electromagnetic radiation from equipment such as mobile phones and microwave ovens
- A faraday cage can be used in some circumstances to eliminate EMRs from a room
- Good ventilation prevents and inhibits toxic mould growth
- Employing passive climate control methods in the house will reduce the need for treated ducted air in buildings. This in turn improves the micro climate
- Reduce chemical exposure as much as possible
- The more 'green' elements we employ, the less power we use, and the less we pollute our atmosphere

Any environment that can potentially make us ill will more than likely disrupt sleep. Good health depends on the environment as well as the state of our mind and body. We can eat all the right foods and do lots of exercise but if we are constantly exposed to EMR and pollutants from toxic materials, these factors will work against our immune system.

If you suspect that you are suffering from the effects of building emissions, a visit to your natural health practitioner such as a homoeopath, naturopath, Ayurvedic practitioner or Chinese medicine specialist is wise as they will give treatments that detoxify your body and provide advice as to how to take measures to improve your indoor climate.

Chapter 12

Working Nights

> *Me thought I heard a voice cry, Sleep no more:*
> *Macbeth does murder sleep.*
>
> – William Shakespeare (1606)

There are few barriers to working round the clock these days. Many goods and services are produced and delivered 24/7 as they strive to make profit in competitive global markets.

And of course there are some professions such as the police, fire authorities and medical professionals who need to provide on-going care as they are busy looking after people who are suffering from the consequences of overwork and stress.

The unfortunate reality is that some people have to work shifts that go into and through the night. Shift work plays havoc with the body clock and can cause the following problems:

- Uncontrollable or unintentional sleep episodes – not a good look being face down in your breakfast
- Difficulty focusing and maintaining attention – people think you do not care
- Decreased performance at work and home – causes tension when you do not do your share of the housework
- Increase in job, home or traffic accidents – pain!
- Having to take more frequent naps at home or at work – asleep in charge of a forklift might be a cause for concern
- Difficulty treating a medical or mental illness – immunity and tolerance levels are low

Early recognition of any of the above signs can be the first step in preventing a more serious, chronic condition that can result from a compromised immune system.

If a sleep disorder is suspected, a sleep diary is a helpful way to assist the evaluation of the quality and quantity of sleep.

Individual Strategies for a Better Life on Shift Work

Make the most out of the opportunities when you can sleep by following good sleep hygiene. Develop habits that encourage sleep and have those sleeps at optimum times in the circadian cycle.

A Room with no View

- Whether you are sleeping in the day or night, make your sleeping environment quiet, dark and comfortable. Try to block out the sounds of the day as much as you can

Ingest for Rest

- Reduce or eliminate consumption of stimulants such as caffeine and nicotine
- Eat a healthy diet and take good nutritious food to work rather than high sugar snacks. High sugar snacks will make you exhausted and unfocused after a few hours
- Large meals should not be consumed too close to bedtime after a night shift

Sleeping to Schedule

- Make sure that your family maintains their routines so that life can go on as normal
- Because working at night puts you at a disadvantage socially. Try scheduling meals with other members of the family and friends so that relationships are fostered and you do not lose touch with your world. This might mean eating breakfast while your family is having dinner
- Allow yourself sleeping periods whenever you can. This might mean sleeping in split periods, which is better than having no sleep. A split sleep means sleeping for 3-4 hours just before work and 3-4 hours immediately after. This works well if you are able to sleep for a part of the night, which is when your body expects to be asleep
- On your days off, do not revert back to normal sleeping patterns as it will confuse your brain too much. Use a technique called 'anchor sleep'. This means that you still sleep for some of the time that you would during your working week. So if during the working week you sleep from 8 am-2 pm then on your days off sleep from 3 am-11 am. The time from 8 am-11 am is your anchor sleep. This

means there is time to be with friends and family while maintaining the sleep routine
- Do not nap at random times. This can make it harder to establish a regular sleeping program. Routine is important to sleep quality regardless of the schedule you work on. Just as daytime napping for non-shift workers can disrupt night time sleep; it can also make it harder for shift workers to sleep during planned sleep periods

Lifesavers

- On the other hand, having a brief snooze before you drive home from work could save your life
- Shift workers should consider catching public transport home as sleep deprivation affects cognitive ability and concentration and, as we know, significantly enhances the risk of accidents

Reset the Body Clock

- Melatonin could be a useful tool for a shift worker. Melatonin is the sleep hormone secreted naturally at night by the pineal gland in response to darkness. Just as for jet lag, melatonin has been shown to hasten the resetting of circadian rhythms in certain circumstances and it has a sedating effect

Fit for Sleep

- Regular exercise will improve the general mood and promote alertness on night shifts. It has been shown to increase circadian adaptation as well. Aerobic exercise done immediately after waking is most effective no matter which shift you work. However, do not exercise too close to bedtime because it will stimulate you

Importantly, people who work shifts need understanding family and friends. It is easy for shift workers to feel a sense of isolation from the worlds of their loved ones.

Tips for Employers

Shift work is a strain that family life does not always bear well. Add to that the increased risk of heart disease, high blood pressure, ulcers and stomach upsets and of course sleep disorders.

Studies conducted by the Circadian Learning Centre in America also showed that night shift workers around the world were more likely to become obese due to unusual eating habits and lack of exercise, they had a higher divorce rate, abused drugs and alcohol more often and suffered depression.

Understandably working when you are meant to be sleeping increases risks to workplace safety and these risks spill over to a person's personal life. Following are some handy tips for employers to help create a healthier work environment:

- Provide proper lighting, adequate ventilation and comfortable temperatures. These factors contribute to safety and facilitate greater productivity because people will feel fresher and more awake
- Make the dining room spacious and comfortable with space for people to enjoy social interaction. Serve only nutritious food as fast food will deplete the health of staff and make them more likely to be listless and tired
- Also stock vending machines with nutritious foods. Drinks that contain high levels of sugar and stimulants will cause staff to be more tired than ever
- If there is space, a place to nap will be beneficial
- Provide exercise facilities and equipment along with scheduled time to use them

- Offer counselling and support groups. Shift work will bring its own set of challenges. There are the effects of poor sleep habits, plus possible feelings of isolation because they are not engaging at 'normal' times with family and friends. So there is the risk of psychological disorders such as depression and anxiety
- In industries where employees do complicated or high risk jobs, make use of expert consultants who can assist with appropriate scheduling for rest and sleep, and create nutrition strategies

Nurses

Ironically those who work in the caring profession are themselves at risk when it comes to personal health, especially those who work at night, and at day and night shifts.

Various studies have been carried out on the effects of shift work on nurses. One found that nurses who slept five hours or less a night had an almost 40 per cent higher chance of developing heart disease than colleagues who got eight hours sleep at night. An American study found that nurses who worked rotating shifts for six years had a 51 per cent greater risk of a heart attack than those on day shift.

Another study found that people who had only four hours sleep per night for six nights developed decreased glucose tolerance, which is a precursor to diabetes.

Helpful hints for nurses include:
- Sleep and eat well before your shift
- Wear a 24 hour digital watch to keep from being disoriented about night and day
- Eat balanced meals with complex carbohydrates combined with some protein and moderate amounts of fat

✦ Eat or drink something warm if hormonal changes make you feel especially chilled

Nursing is intrinsically a hazardous occupation. A nurse is exposed to infectious diseases, being constantly on their feet, emotional trauma, back injury due to heavy lifting and a host of other hazards so they need to be resilient. Inappropriate sleep will affect their ability to cope mentally and physically with these sorts of demands.

Chapter 13

Lifestyles of the Tired and Restless

Taking Account of Lifestyle

Graham, an accountant, wakes up at 6 am and does a long day at work. He gets home at around 7 pm and does some more work on his investment portfolio and has dinner at 8 pm without taking time out to relax.

He drinks coffee throughout the day and by evening he has a lot of sugar in his diet. Graham loves cake. He is overweight and highly strung although he has a façade of calm. Because he cannot sleep at night. He falls asleep watching television on the weekends, and he suffers from migraine.

Recently Graham took up yoga. This is a step towards a more balanced lifestyle and he is really enjoying it. With this extra awareness of mind and body, his sleep patterns are starting to improve.

***

The way we live has a strong impact on our state of health. Do you live like Graham with no boundaries to your work life or do you watch television in bed, have a glass of wine or whisky to help send you off to sleep or drink coffee in the evening? These are not great habits if you want to develop or maintain good sleep patterns.

Or you may sleep well most of the time but have the occasional bout of insomnia.

As an insurance policy against developing a more chronic form of sleeplessness it would be wise to make some modifications to your sleep habits, which do not just refer to bedtime. Good habits for sleep also involve what we do during the day.

Having squeaky clean sleep hygiene is not difficult to achieve, it is just a matter of being willing to adopt them.

Sleeping is Habit Forming

Stupidity is doing the same thing over and over again while expecting a different outcome. If you continue with poor habits it is unlikely that you will achieve the good sleep you need. This would be poor sleep hygiene.

Electric bedrooms

The following should be eliminated from the bed chamber:

- Televisions emit electromagnetic radiation. Watching it before sleep can be stimulating
- An impending alarm from an alarm clock can encourage constant waking to check the time. Waking up to a loud alarm is stressful and wakes us up in fright because of the suddenness and shock of the noise. If you are regularly getting enough sleep, then you should not need an alarm

because you will naturally wake up at the same time each day
+ Electrical devices such as any kind of phone chargers emit damaging electromagnetic radiation

Regular bedtime

+ As often as possible, go to bed at the same time each night. The body clock regulates sleep and getting out of the sleep routine means it needs resetting
+ Establishing a consistent sleep schedule will synchronise your biological clock. Therefore, your biological clock will promote sleep and waking at the right times (added bonus is money saved by not buying an alarm clock).
+ Wake up at the same time every morning, even on the weekend. This will tell your brain to release sleep/wake hormones at the right time
+ Our adrenal glands do the majority of their recovering during the hours of 10 pm-2 am so it is best to go to bed early

If you have a late night and you try to make up for the lost sleep by either sleeping in, taking a nap or going to bed early this will disrupt the regularity of the body clock and create sleep difficulties the next night. Instead go to bed at the normal time the following night to re-establish your sleep pattern.

Creating a Peaceful Pre-sleep Space

What you do before hitting the sack is as important as what you do when you get to bed. Violent, suspenseful television shows before bed will stress you and infect your psyche. You are more likely not to sleep well because of restless dreams.

If you hop into bed straight after a long session of work then you will probably have difficulty falling asleep because you are stimulated. No matter how tired you are, when your head hits the pillow you may find yourself suddenly wide awake. That is frustrating.

The brain and body need time to wind down and enter a relaxed state that promotes sleep. If you are working at night put the work away at least an hour before bed so your mind has time to unwind and do not get into bed while you feel anxious about work.

What not to do in the Bedroom

+ Have intense discussions or arguments
+ Talk business or indulge in intellectual discourse
+ Watch television
+ Use a computer
+ Do your accounts

Are you getting the picture? The bedroom needs to be a haven away from pressure, a place for peaceful sleep

Before going to bed, employ restful and relaxing rituals. Here are some suggestions:

+ Knit or crochet something
+ A crossword or Sudoku puzzle will take your mind off the day's stress
+ Take a warm bath with a few drops of relaxing essential oils such as lavender around an hour before bedtime. (Refer to aromatherapy section page (see page 193). A bath warms you up and relaxes you*
+ Read an inspirational or meditative story. This will transport your mind to a peaceful place

---

*Your body temperature needs to fall for you to feel sleepy. The bath actually helps lower your temperature because the warm water artificially raises your body temperature, which then comes down once you are out of the bath.

- Listen to soft, gentle music, rainforest sounds or spiritual gandharva veda music
- Do yogic breathing exercises and stretches to relax your neck, shoulders, back and abdomen
- Burn relaxing aromatherapy oils such as lavender
- Pray
- Recite positive affirmations

Setting the Scene for Sleep

Sweet Thoughts Make Sweet Dreams

Bring to your bed the nicest thoughts because if you are going to be thinking of something before going to sleep it might as well be something pleasant.

If it has been a rough day, consciously turn your cogitations to your fondest memories, times when you felt warm and secure. Recall happy childhood events, a time when sleep was a pleasurable experience that your brain gently embraced, or imagine a wonderful holiday lying under a palm tree on a pristine beach. Train your mind to bring those kind of thoughts to the fore instead of the ones that cause you worry and anxiety.

Lights, Melatonin, Sleep

- Lighting, or rather the lack of it is very important when it comes to sleep because melatonin, the sleep hormone that prepares your brain for sleep, needs diminishing levels of light to help its manufacture
- Bright light or staring at your laptop computer will likely delay the effect. Prior to sleeping, keep the lights in your bedroom low

Create the Right Bedroom Environment

The bedroom should be a sacrosanct space used solely for sleep and love.

- Use your bed and bedroom only for sleeping or intimate relations. It should be a restful environment and comfortable. Have it as dark as possible. Work and recreational items such as televisions, computers and phones should not be in the bedroom. Do not watch television, work or eat in bed. If you are used to watching television or doing work in bed, you may find it harder to relax and to think of the bed as a place to sleep

- When it is time for lights out, the room needs to be quiet and dark so that melatonin can do its thing. Remember that light can disrupt the circadian rhythm and the pineal glands production of melatonin and serotonin. Sleep in as close to complete darkness as possible. If the curtains do not keep light out, consider an eye mask

- The bedroom should not be too hot. Keep the temperature no higher than 22 degrees. A hot bedroom is dehydrating and likely to wake you up reaching for a glass of water. Then of course you will need to go to the toilet

- Every part of the night time experience should be rest enhancing, including a comfortable, back supporting bed with the right bedding

- It is not a good idea to sleep with your beloved cat or dog as they can wake you up during the night just because they feel like nuzzling your nose

- Go to the bathroom just before going to bed to reduce your chances of waking up to go in the middle of night

Bedroom – brown, Pink or Blue?

You could paint the town red but it might be best not to paint the bedroom that colour. Red produces feelings of excitement so a person who has a heart complaint, or someone who is stressed and irritable, should not sleep in a red room.

Red is an expansive colour that opens up the heart. This is reflected in society's depiction of the heart with the colour red. So for some, a red feature wall might be appropriate.

There is much power in colour. Good colours for the bedroom are generally neutral relaxing tones.

According to Feng Shui, colour is applied according to your individual constitution and the five elements fire, earth, metal, water and wood. Each of these elements has colours attributed to them that when prescribed correctly can maximise your life potential and aid good sleep and health.

A Feng Shui practitioner can determine the appropriate directions for you to sleep, which includes your personal power, area and your bedroom's 'elemental' colour.

I'm Trying to Sleep

Some people have the ability to sleep even under the noisiest of circumstances, whether it be noise in the house, or your neighbours' barking dogs, crowing roosters, or worse still, a deluded Elvis wanna-be neighbour with a karaoke machine.

However many of us are unable to emotionally detach from exterior noise, so sleeping under such circumstances can be a big challenge.

Some Effective Ways to Block Out Din

- Ear plugs can help although they do not completely eliminate sound. There are also products on the market such as an eye and ear mask that block both sight and sound
- An effective method is to play 'white noise'. Just as white light is made up of all the colours of the spectrum, white noise, or flat noise, is made up of all the frequencies and sound wavelengths in the sound spectrum. If it is played at the same time as other noises are occurring such as a barking dog, those noises blend with the white noise and become indistinguishable so the only thing a person will hear is a gentle soothing hum
- Listen to a CD of chanting or a beautiful background noise that you do not focus on such as the sea. There are many relaxation CDs on the market that play everything from whale song and forest noises to womb sounds
- Listen to a CD with theta waves, which are the brain waves that occur when we are in deep sleep

Still cannot Sleep?

If it is one of those nights where you just cannot fall asleep, do not lie in bed contemplating life and the universe as you are likely to become even more agitated. Get up for a while and use some of your rituals to assist your body back into the sleep mode. Then return to bed when you feel ready to sleep.

Some Useful Ways to Prepare Yourself for Sleep

- Have a cup of warm milk with some honey. Science has shown that the tryptophan in milk helps create drowsiness. Adding a bit of honey makes tryptophan work quicker as the presence of this naturally derived sugar speeds up the process

- Dab your temples with some lavender oil (adults only; not suitable for children)
- Meditate
- Read a spiritual story
- If something is bothering you or you keep going over something in your mind, try clearing your thoughts by writing the problem down. Alternatively talk to someone you trust such as a family member or a professional counselor. This can help release the difficult feelings you may be experiencing.

Clouding Troubling Thoughts

Another useful way to rid yourself of troublesome thoughts is to do a visualisation exercise. While lying in bed with your eyes closed, picture the problem you are having and place it in a coloured cloud. It could be pink or purple, whatever colour comes to mind.

Then let the cloud go. Send it off with love and watch as it drifts away taking the problem with it into space. Allow yourself to drift into a peaceful sleep.

***

Substances Affecting Sleep

Stimulants

Some people are sensitive to caffeine and even small amounts will contribute to insomnia. It is best to avoid caffeine after lunchtime. This is because caffeine is not metabolized efficiently in the body so most people still feel the effects long after consuming it. Coffee is also a dehydrator so it is very important that if you drink coffee you also replenish your water stores. Although it is important to remain hydrated, drinking excess water before bed may also disrupt sleep.

Alcohol

While alcohol may make you feel drowsy and hasten the time taken to fall asleep, the effect is short-lived. Many people find that they wake during the night and cannot fall back sleep. This is because blood alcohol levels drop and wake you up later in the night.

Alcohol also stops you falling into the deeper stages of sleep where the body does most of its healing.

If you use alcohol as a means to fall asleep you can build a tolerance to the sleep inducing effect so you may need more alcohol to produce the same effect. So avoid using alcohol to help you get to sleep.

It is interesting to note that if you have had five nights of sleep deprivation, drinking three alcoholic drinks will have the same effect on your body as six alcoholic drinks would have on a non sleep deprived individual.

Food

If you are sensitive to certain foods such as dairy and wheat products, avoid them. Food sensitivities can affect sleep and even cause symptoms such as apnoea, congestion, night sweats, gastrointestinal upsets and wind.

Medications

Some prescription and over the counter medications can effect sleep because they can be stimulating or have side effects. The better our state of health, the less need there will be to use them.

Exercise

Regular exercise enhances well-being. Doing some form of exercise for at least 30 minutes every day will also assist you to fall asleep. Studies show that exercising is best in the morning.

No heavy exercise regime should be employed any more than six hours before bedtime.

Vigilance

If you feel a sleep problem coming on, do not wait to seek professional help.

Be aware of what your body is telling you when you are going through a rough patch with a relationship or experiencing problems at work that cause a few sleepless nights because a few sleepless nights have the potential to turn into many.

If the insomnia persists for more than a week-get help. Early intervention may prevent or reduce the need for 'a pound of cure.'

To sleep perchance to learn, Weary with toil,
I haste to my bed, The dear repose
For limbs with travel tired;
But then begins, A journey in my head
To work my mind, When body's works expire.

– William Shakespeare,
Sonnet 27 (1609)

Bedding Down

So impactful is the quality of our bedding that it has the ability to give us a sore back, a pain in the neck and a lousy night's sleep.

The mattress is the most important item and the pillow is the finishing touch.

If money is no issue then buy the best bedding you can. This is an investment in your health, and the bigger the bed the better from a comfort perspective, especially if you do not sleep alone. People turn and move constantly throughout the night and if you sleep with someone who has those wriggly legs, you will be grateful for the opportunity of distance.

Discover Your Inner Spring

When buying a mattress, no matter which kind, be it made from latex, springs or memory foam, test it well in the store to make sure it provides enduring support. Do not be afraid to have a good practical lie down and ask enough questions to send the sales person off to have a rest on the nearest sleeping slab.

For instance, when purchasing a spring mattress consider the number and type of coils. A mattress with thicker and more plentiful coils placed in locations where your body requires the most support, such as the curve in your lumbar spine*, is best.

A mattress needs to support the neck, shoulders, hips, lower back and legs. Your spine should be straight when you lie on your side and maintain its natural curve when you lie on your back.

On a more scientific level, Isaac Newton's third law of motion states that every action is opposed by an equal and opposite reaction. Therefore, a mattress will compress further where there is greater weight; it needs to accommodate the person's weight curve-from head to thighs-in order to support and minimise stress.

---

*The lumbar spine is the lower part of the back that bears much of your body weight.

So, the more you increase the surface area of contact between the body and the bed the less pressure the body is being subjected to. This is what you want to achieve when choosing a mattress.

Most mattresses are made for the 'average' person so they may not provide support in the right places for everyone. And do not forget your partner, if you have one; you may need to consider two very different body shapes and sizes needing support.

There are many different kinds of mattresses in the market of varying quality and they all provide different levels of support; some are made from latex which is made from the sap of rubber trees. There are innovative ergonomic beds and mattresses that do not forget you because they are made from 'memory foam'.

Memory foam mattresses conform to your body shape and apply pressure in places of least resistance such as your lumbar spine. It is made from viscoelastic material (polyurethane) and was developed by NASA for use by astronauts to relieve the effects of G-forces.

The material moulds to the body's contours providing optimal support to blast you off into a blissful sleep. It is a material that is affected by heat. It softens and becomes malleable so you sink into it more. However, memory foam can be much firmer in cold weather making it harder to create a cavity. You need to make sure that it has the right level of density.

Spring mattresses have their own set of merits and these depend on the number, place, shape and gauge of the springs so do not be afraid to ask a few 'coiling' questions.

Softer foam mattresses might feel great initially, but since they do not provide sufficient support for your lumbar spine, expect the development of some aches and pains.

Water beds are not recommended because water conducts electricity so they become a source of electromagnetic radiation.

And for those who like the element of asymmetry in the bedroom, be mindful that round shaped beds can make you feel like you are in perpetual motion, which can cause you not to feel relaxed and secure in bed.

The lifespan of a mattress is approximately 8-10 years like a fridge but not so frosty. They will last for this long if they are made out of durable materials.

Pillow Talk

The best way to sleep is either on your back or side in order to support the neck and back.

Everyone is physically different, so our pillow preferences vary. Some people like no pillow, some flat pillows and others sleep with two or more pillows. However, the right pillow can help us sleep more deeply and because of the comfort we experience through being well aligned, we will be less likely to toss and turn during the night.

Pillow purchasing should be as thorough a process as for a mattress. Lie down on a pillow for 15 minutes or longer to test the comfort level.

Comfort is not the only criteria of a good pillow. People with allergies should avoid polyester and feather pillows; latex is less allergenic because of its anti-microbial qualities.

The Fairy Tale Phenomenon

Pillows made from latex feel firm and heavy to hold but when you put your head down on them, they have the Goldilocks affect; they do not feel too hard or too soft, they feel just right!

Latex is long lasting and resistant to dust mites, mould and mildew. It holds its shape and is suitable for people who sleep on their side or back as the contour shape fills the gap between the neck and shoulders. However, its bounciness is not to everyone's liking. Be aware that the quality of latex varies and it can become sticky and uncomfortable in hot climates.

Pillows from Space

Pillows made from memory foam have a unique asymmetrical shape with a shoulder curve on one edge that is designed to fill the hollow created between the head and shoulders. This makes it perfect for side sleepers. The lower flat surface on the other edge suits back and stomach sleepers and those who have an average to larger sized body.

Traditional Pillows

Feather and down pillows offer a sense of luxury as one sinks into them. They last up to eight years but provide relatively poor support. They are not appropriate for people with allergies.

The common or garden synthetic, polyester pillows made from spun fiber, microfiber or hollow fiber are the most common types. Polyester pillows need to be replaced every six months.

Pioneering Pillows

A quadra zone pillow provides the option of four zones to lay your head in to keep your neck and spine in natural alignment. Zone 1 supports the natural curve of the neck, zone 2 is the soft mid section that cradles the main weight of the head and zones 3 and 4 are the medium density side wings that are ideal for people who sleep on their sides.

It is filled with fluffy polyester balls that move independently of each other and are easily pumped up. It suits average to larger framed people and those who prefer a thicker pillow.

Special Need Pillows

'Cervical' or 'orthopedic' pillows are contoured to take up the space under the head and neck and are helpful for those who have neck pain and backache because they help to keep the neck and spine aligned.

These pillow types have a deeper depression where the head lies and extra support under the neck. They are also helpful for snorers, pregnant women and people who suffer from reflux.
Some orthopedic pillows wear out after one or two years.

Allergy Dust Mite Protectors

A pillow gains up to half its weight in dust mites and their faeces. After that smattering of information you will surely be thrilled to know that there are dust mite protectors for pillows.

No Nightmare Nightwear

The fabric of the garments you wear to bed also impact health and sleep. What you put on your body can be as important as what you put in your body when it comes to good health.

Bed clothing should be comfortable. A lot of cheap clothing is made from man-made fibers and produced with chemicals such as formaldehyde, which can adversely affect your health. These can cause allergies and other negative health side effects.

Purchasing 100 per cent organic cotton, silk and hemp sleep wear, bedding and linen will allow the skin to breathe while sleeping. These fabrics are safe and comfortable options.

Chapter 14

Sleeping During Stressful Times

Schools in

If you believe that our time on earth is like being in a classroom, where we are challenged to think, learn and grow as spiritual beings, then it can give more meaning to the fact that we have so many 'lessons' placed before us; some of which are very challenging and difficult to negotiate our way through.

Stress runs far deeper than just emotion; it also refers to a biological response. It is the consequence of the failure of a human or animal to respond healthily to emotional or physical threats, whether real or imagined.

The stress response is 'autonomic', which means it is a biological response to an environmental stimulus that we cannot control. Our body goes into a state of alarm causing us to produce adrenaline. This is the 'flight or fight' mechanism.

Common stress symptoms include:
- Irritability
- Muscular tension
- Inability to concentrate
- Physical reactions such as headaches and elevated heart rate

The breadth of stressful experiences is wide. At the extreme end there is war and imprisonment, grief and loss from the death of loved ones. Then there are the day to day stresses such as work deadlines and dealing with traffic.

Other major stressors include:
- Relationship breakups
- Abuse
- Grief
- Money
- Parenting issues
- Job losses
- Relationship conflicts
- Illness
- Moving house
- Boredom
- Exams
- Environmental stress caused by pollution, poor working conditions, noise and light

Our responses during these experiences or lessons are important to consider because they give us the opportunity to reflect on ourselves and the self beliefs that might not serve us well.

Do not Panic!

In certain circumstances stress may be a positive experience. It can prompt the activation of internal resources to meet challenges and achieve goals. However, negative stress is in fact a problem that plagues the modern era and is a major contributor to mental, physical and social problems throughout the world.

City living causes stress and sleep debts. We sleep less than we did a century ago and the noise of cities and towns has a profound effect on the nervous system.

The modern world is consumed with the desire for more luxuries like houses, cars, holidays and recreational equipment so debt levels are soaring. In Australia alone, debt levels have never been higher so people feel pressure to work longer hours; hence they spend less time with their families.

In this case the stressor is the disparity between reality and fantasy, that is, how our life actually is and how we would really like it to be. And the physical and mental responses or symptoms are very real. The 'flight or fight' response, where stress hormones are released, is an acute response to stress, and these in turn cause around 1,500 physical and mental responses as the body rallies itself into action in order to deal with a perceived threat.

Add to this increased use of alcohol and recreational and pharmaceutical drugs amongst wide sections of populations, and the lack of spirituality, social and community connection and life philosophies, and you have a recipe for deep and sustained stress.

Stress is also a response to the unknown and change as well as demands and difficulties. We know that a little bit of stress can be a good thing when we have to get something done. Our adrenalin pumps, we are focused and not easily distracted.

However, too much stress, particularly over a long period, can be a bad thing. It can cause us to freeze up; we feel overwhelmed and unable to cope. It can also compromise our immune system, which can lead to illness.

All these actions and events have the potential to impact our health and sleeping patterns.

Stressed people take their worries to bed. And people who cannot sleep stress about not being able to fall asleep.

We know that without a decent night's sleep we have a decreased ability to cope with the normal daily activities and it is even more vital that we have all our resources in tact when we are dealing with greater challenges.

Inbred Stress

Adrenalin Rush

Do you know people who 'live on their nerves'? There is intensity in every activity they undertake and it takes only the slightest of irregularities to cause a stress episode. Even making a cup of tea is carried out with muscles tensed and brow furrowed. These people are very hard to spend time with because their stress levels are infectious.

This kind of chronic stress actually becomes ingrained because the hormonal systems that trigger the flight or fight response have the capability of being programmed. Stress feeds on stress and the adrenalin release becomes a habit that the body learns and eventually it is hardwired as a behaviour pattern. In time, if the stress mechanism is not dealt with, the body reacts quicker and more forcefully to a stressor.

Signs of Stress

Because we are all different, the way each individual responds to stress varies. Notice how your family members come home after a difficult day at work or school. The kids might be grumpy and when asked about their day, give a monosyllabic answer. On returning home from work Dad might head straight for his study and need to withdraw for a while in order to wind down before facing the family.

These kinds of signs are worth noting and pursuing at a time when the person is feeling more able to communicate. Being able to talk about a stressor can help a person deal with an issue. Remember the old saying, 'a problem shared is a problem halved.'

Following are a list of symptoms that commonly result from stress. How do you rate yourself against these symptoms?

Table 14.1

Affect	Symptoms	Your Answer
Moods and attitudes	1. Do you become withdrawn, moody, irritable, restless and impatient? 2. Does your mood swing from one extreme to the other? 3. Do you lack enthusiasm? 4. Are you disinterested in your usual hobbies and activities? 5. Are you seeing less of your friends?	
Performance	1. Are you performing below your normal abilities? 2. Is your energy low?	
Eating patterns	1. Are you eating to try and make yourself feel better (comfort eating)? 2. Have you stopped eating regularly and have no appetite? 3. Have your eating patterns changed?	

Sleeping	1. Are your sleeping patterns either less or more? 2. Is your sleep disturbed or erratic?	
Overall health	1. Are you feeling generally unwell?	
Behaviour	1. Do you engage in more risk taking behaviour than usual such as being less careful while driving?	

Breathe in, Breathe out, Breathe in...

Stress can lead to anxiety and anxiety can lead to panic attacks. Panic attacks can be caused by or be a result of hyperventilation, which is in turn caused by anxiety.

Hyperventilation causes the following physical symptoms:

+ Difficulty breathing
+ Dizziness
+ Feeling faint
+ Being unable to talk
+ Tingling in the fingers
+ Pain in the chest

Pouring Salt on the Wound

One of the physiological consequences of the stress of modern life is that our body uses up the mineral salts and vitamins necessary for energy and concentration. This lack can cause depression, insomnia, irritability and feelings of anger and rage.

If you are experiencing any of these stress symptoms then it is time to think about what is happening in your life in order to plan ways to take control. This takes three steps:

1. Acknowledge that you are stressed
2. Find ways to reduce the stressors
3. Establish coping mechanisms to manage, process and eliminate stress

Stress, be Gone!

Generally, people who are stressed for whatever reason tend to get less than the required eight hours of sleep.

What happens when we are stressed is that our brain can become overactive as we attempt to think hard about how to solve the stressor. This thinking time can be especially acute when we stop our work and activities for the day and lay our head on the pillow to sleep.

Now, there is a hint in that last statement. If time has not been spent winding down in preparation for sleep then the stressed and over stimulated brain continues its chatter, despite tiredness and exhaustion.

Also, you may eventually get to sleep but find yourself waking through the night with a problem rolling through your head. It is very frustrating when you cannot switch off!

Dealing with stressful scenarios requires a concerted effort.

If you are going through a stressful period do not let it continue and build to the point where it becomes ingrained. Find ways to alleviate and deal with the issue in a more appropriate way and find ways to create more personal resilience to stressful situations.

Some Helpful Ideas

+ Find a way to deal with the cause of the stress. If it is a work related problem you need to work out a way to solve it, preferably during work hours, not while in bed. If it is

about relationships and it is an ongoing issue, then it might be worthwhile getting some impartial assistance from a counsellor
- People who work long hours often tend to use more caffeine to get them through a long work session. This will affect sleep
- During times of stress maintaining your health will take some extra effort because stress reduces your immunity, so diet, time out, meditation and work/recreation balance is especially important. Regular exercise and relaxation techniques can reduce stress and build coping skills
- Practice good sleep hygiene. Do not turn off the computer and then hop straight into bed. Take some time to do something relaxing that takes you away from whatever has consumed you during the day
- Psychological problems can be tackled in various ways including counselling and meditation. Finding the joy of life through activities that are satisfying to your soul such as hobby activities like painting, sculpting, sewing, woodwork or making model airplanes. Having a creative outlet is important
- If we do not already feel good about ourselves then we need to explore why and work towards understanding that our value does not lie in the way we look, what we do for a living or any other external factor
- To manage stress we also need to examine our priorities and evaluate what is and is not working for us in terms of our relationships with family, work, social life, career, health and finances
- Work towards removing sources of excess stress from your life. It is worth noting that you may not be able to

remove a stressful situation. However, you can modify your responses to the circumstances

- ✦ Contemplate the values we hold dear and assess the appropriateness of our goals and how we measure success
- ✦ Create space and time every day for self nurture. This will vary according to what you consider to be nurturing. For some it might be having a massage, for others it could be watching comedy DVDs
- ✦ Creating emotional place or physical distance from a stressful event can provide perspective and help us see our way through solving an issue, which can be difficult if you are caught in the middle of it. There are many ways to create that distance; watch a movie, go for a holiday, bake a cake or paint a picture
- ✦ Spending some time in nature is good for our health and soul. It should be something we factor into our week; whether it is visiting the seaside, walks in the park or gardening
- ✦ It is most important that we have a laugh and have fun! Joy is a great healer
- ✦ Providing you are not allergic to animal fur, pets are wonderful companions that offer unconditional love. They help us relax and we have fun as we laugh at their antics. Spending time with animals is even therapeutic as pets have the ability to lower blood pressure

We are What We Imagine

Anxiety and stress can also be brought about by feeling that we are not in control of our life and unable to have free choice in particular situations.

The more we stress and think negative thoughts the deeper our tension becomes and we can catch ourselves spiraling down into a negative thought pattern. It takes a bit of effort but it can be helpful to try and take control by refocusing the mind on uplifting and positive thoughts and images.

The first thing we need to do is to be aware of our thought patterns. We need to consciously stop when we begin engaging in negative thinking and refocus our thoughts.

Visualising something uplifting and positive helps us to feel and return to calm and it assists us to gain perspective. And, importantly, the body follows the mind in relation to thoughts.

Supplements and Remedies Helpful for Stress

The following supplements can be useful in the management of stress. Check with a health professional such as a naturopath to find the best treatment and make sure you combine it with other previous suggestions.

- Magnesium and potassium phosphoid in colloid form
- Vitamin B complex
- Herbs such as withania, passiflora, lavender, hops, valerian and vervain
- Skullcap, chamomile, kava, oats seed can be taken as a herbal complex or as individual substances
- Flower essences such as vervain, impatiens, hornbeam, mimulus
- There are homoeopathic drops that can assist with releasing stress
- Diet is another important factor as people under stress often skip meals, drink too much coffee and eat takeaway food.

Instead they should start with a good breakfast including cereal (sugar free!), proteins such as baked beans, eggs and wholemeal bread. Include some protein and vegetables* in the lunch and do not eat dinner late. A body properly fuelled will be more resilient to stress

✦ Protein contains amino acids, which are needed for neurotransmitter production. Protein helps brain function so it is important to have small amounts of good quality protein with every meal to help the body regulate the stress response

Post-traumatic Stress

Many people find themselves dealing with a traumatic event at some stage of their lives. It is a tragic fact of life that many people live in war torn countries where they or their loved ones may suffer some form of extreme violence.

There are also certain professions that are more likely to come across shocking events such as the military, police, medical profession and ambulance officers.

Post-traumatic stress can also be suffered by people because of a car accident or the experience of a disaster or being diagnosed with an illness that is potentially fatal. Any experience that causes great shock can engender the experience of helplessness or fear and horror that the mind has much difficulty making sense of. It is common to relive the experiences constantly, which in turn can cause anxiety, panic attacks, phobias and other psychological conditions.

Much of the time people work out a way to deal with the problem and are able to get on with their lives but for some, it leaves

---

*Have five servings of vegetables a day and three servings of fruit.

deep scars that are quite incapacitating. This is called post-traumatic stress disorder (PTSD).

PTSD and Sleep

Often people in this state experience nightmares about the event and have difficulty falling and staying asleep. There are a number of ways to deal with PTSD. Here are a few suggestions:

+ Psychological counselling where the person learns how to deal with their emotions and manage anger, anxiety and depression
+ Natural medicine
+ Hypnosis
+ Learning to release the visions that constantly play in their brain

It is time now to shed the constraints of stress and sleeplessness to explore the techniques and tools that will help you relinquish the tossing and turning, snoring and skin crawling.

CHAPTER 15

Natural Therapies Explained

Most natural therapies come from the point of view of returning the overall functioning of an individual to a state of homoeostasis. However, not all modalities may be capable of doing that in and of themselves. You may need to use a combination. Finding the right combination can often be a challenge.

Natural therapy is a broad title. It can encompass any number of healing modalities and the approach of many natural therapists is to work with the patient to find the remedy that is going to best suit the patient's temperament and area of difficulty. They are not necessarily going to prescribe medicines, herbal or otherwise.

The therapist examines the person eclectically, as a whole entity, mind, body and spirit. They work on the paradigm that balance needs to be restored in the body, not that a disease needs to be healed. For example, it may take art therapy in conjunction with body therapies and counselling to restore that balance. The natural therapist or holistic doctor recognises the importance of the humanising element of healing, that is, that the patient needs to feel, listened to and heard.

Ill Health Can be an Opportunity

Insomnia, disease or illness relays a message telling us that we need to closely question our lifestyle and evaluate the changes necessary to find health and harmony. If we understand that emotional or physical disease is not a random event then perhaps we can see it as a gift.

Therefore, the symptoms of disease demand that we question and create a new paradigm that includes the following elements:

- How we take care of ourselves
- Our attitudes
- The values we hold as important
- The direction we are taking in life
- Our spiritual needs

Whatever challenges present themselves to us are an opportunity to examine an aspect of ourselves so that we can face the issue and deal with it. That way we do not have to keep on experiencing the same kind of difficulties over and over. This helps us to grow.

For example, if we keep ignoring a pain and take a pain killer then we are not approaching the root cause of the pain in order to try and fix it, so chances are it will get worse. It is the same with our emotions. If we keep burying something deep in our psyche then whenever we are presented with a situation that challenges that idea or feeling about ourselves, it comes up to tell us again that this is hurting us and needs attention.

Often people are perplexed about what to do when faced with ill health. A complete cure will not necessarily be the result of taking prescribed medication or having an operation, although surgery has the ability to release and cut out a myriad of issues in the body.

Why do children have recurring ear infections, why do some people need more than one heart bypass operation and why do people still continue to sleep poorly and feel exhausted during the day even though they take sleeping pills?

We know that a disorder can and often will return unless the genesis of the problem is investigated and the imbalance redressed at all levels—mind, body and spirit.

Natural therapists report that they are usually a last port of call when everything else has been tried and failed and people sometimes report so-called miraculous results after pursuing this course. For instance, children previously prescribed drugs such as Ritalin for ADD or ADHD who move on to homoeopathic medicine, dietary changes, remedial education and body work, do make amazing headway.

Taking a holistic approach to your health means making some different commitments to yourself and your family. Lifestyle change is usually an integral part of healing, which is often the case with a sleep disorder. Changes may be simple or profound, including factors such as diet, relationships and the environment you live and work in.

But healing is not something that we should necessarily do alone and in fact at times a team effort is needed, which could include medical and complementary therapies, although ultimately we need to take responsibility for and be active participants in our healing.

We could blame external sources for our lack of good health. For instance, being around children could be blamed for constantly catching a cold, however, if our immunity is at optimum levels we will be unlikely to catch one no matter how many runny nosed kids we encounter. We can blame our sleeplessness on stress but ultimately it is up to us to take responsibility for the way we handle the stressors and what we do to solve our problems.

This of course is not to say that we are always responsible for a health condition. When one arises it is an opportunity to examine ourselves and ask why we have developed this condition. This way we give ourselves the best chance possible to heal and prevent illness through maintaining optimum emotional, spiritual and physical health. All things being equal, a disease will have nowhere to reside.

Chapter 16

And It's Goodnight From You – Treating Insomnia

The following chapter presents a variety of natural therapy approaches and modalities that can enhance health and treat and prevent sleep problems.

Nutrition

You're Never too Old to Change

Edwina is 88 years old. For 30 years, she complained that she could not sleep through the night. Her diet was poor and she was addicted to sweets. She ate copious amounts of sugar and chocolate throughout the day.

> Her anxiety levels were very high, which was partly related to the amount of sugar she ingested. She ate mostly processed food and minimal servings of fresh greens. Edwina also had a myriad of other health conditions including stomach complaints and constipation.
>
> A naturopath helped Edwina address her diet so her health improved radically. In addition, she taught her visualization and meditation, which helped her to sleep through the night. This impacted positively on her health. After four months of this treatment Edwina felt better than she had when she was in her fifties.

Eating to Sleep

You are what you eat and what your body absorbs. Diet plays an enormous role in the balance of your physical chemistry and in turn can contribute to sleep disorders. Diet certainly played a large part in Edwina's poor health and inability to sleep. Food intolerance, over indulgence and consumption of stimulants such as caffeine can keep you awake or cause poor sleep patterns.

A study has shown that caffeine is not metabolised efficiently in some people so they feel the effects long after consumption. Believe it or not, drinking several cups of coffee in the morning can affect quality of sleep at night. An afternoon cup of coffee (or even tea, which contains more caffeine) will keep some people from falling asleep.

Also, some medications, particularly diet pills contain caffeine.

Understanding your body so that you can know and avoid foods you may be sensitive to is a step in the right direction. Dairy and gluten products can affect sleep and cause apnoea, excess congestion, gastrointestinal upset, bloating and wind.

How to Eat

Eating a heavy meal before bedtime will keep you awake because the body is digesting while it is trying to perform the other vital functions that occur during the resting period. Our digestive system slows at night making it harder to digest late meals.

If you need to eat after dinner time have a high protein snack. Protein is made up of amino acids, which form the building blocks for the production of hormones and neurotransmitters. As you read earlier, certain amino acids such as tryptophan are precursors for melatonin and serotonin, both of which help initiate sleep.

Food intolerance can be a key suspect when considering causes for sleeplessness. Therefore, diet may be especially important in the treatment of sleep disorders.

If there is no other obvious culprit such as unusual stress or a particular illness, explore the possibility of food intolerance.

In a study of infants and sleeplessness, the elimination of cow's milk from the diet and then its reintroduction was a way to determine that there was an allergy to dairy. Some of the most common foods that people are sensitive to are eggs, soy, dairy products, wheat, corn and chocolate.

The sensitivity to the stimulant effects of caffeine varies greatly from one person to the next. This depends on how quickly the body can eliminate caffeine. Even small amounts of caffeine such as those found in decaffeinated coffee or chocolate, may be enough to cause insomnia in some people. Even some tea, such as black and green tea, can stimulate depending on how sensitive a person is.

Wherever possible reduce or eliminate intake of chemicals, preservatives and additives. Anything that has to be described with a number should be avoided at the best of times.

Alcohol produces a number of sleep-impairing effects. In addition to causing the release of adrenaline, alcohol impairs the transport of tryptophan into the brain, and, because the brain is dependent upon tryptophan as the source for serotonin (the important neurotransmitter that initiates sleep), alcohol disrupts serotonin levels.

So if you want to fall asleep more easily, eat a complex carbohydrate snack and a small amount of high protein an hour or two before bed time.

Foods that Aid Sleep

- A handful of walnuts or almonds are a good source of sleep enhancing amino acids
- A piece of turkey, tuna or a small piece of fruit like figs
- Most carbohydrates including bananas. Remember that there are good and bad quality carbohydrates. White bread or biscuits are bad quality carbohydrates
- Plain yoghurt boosts protein levels
- A fruity soya shake is protein rich
- Calcium also helps release serotonin so foods such as milk, broccoli, oats, sesame and sunflower seeds, tahini, raw vegetables, kelp and other seaweeds and watercress
- Be wary of dairy products if you have a sensitivity to them because they tend to increase mucous production

Foods to Avoid at Night

- All soft drinks
- Spicy foods because they can cause heartburn and indigestion
- Alcohol and caffeine in any form including tea, coffee, chocolate
- Monosodium glutamate (MSG), which is often found in Chinese food, causes a stimulant reaction in most people. Symptoms can include heart palpitations, excessive perspiration, dry mouth and migraines

- Refined carbohydrates because they drain the B vitamins. They also contain high levels of sugar, which among other things interferes with mood and hormone levels
- Foods such as cheese, bacon, ham, sausages, eggplant, potatoes, sauerkraut, sugar, tomatoes and wine close to bedtime because they contain tyramine. This is a natural substance that is formed when food ages and breaks down or is fermented. Among other things it increases the release of brain stimulant norepinephrine, which is involved in the fight or flight response
- Foods containing additives or preservatives
- Food containing pesticides
- High protein foods can block the synthesis of serotonin so a large portion of meat is not a good evening food
- Foods high in sugar and refined carbohydrates raise bloodsugar levels and can cause a burst of energy, which we do not want when we are trying to sleep

(See Chapter 19 – Recipes for a good night's sleep for some great recipe ideas.)

'He whose doshas are in balance, whose appetite is good, whose dhatus (tissues) are functioning normally, whose malas (elimination) is in balance and whose self, mind and senses remain full of bliss, is called a healthy person.'
– Definition of a healthy individual according to the ancient Vedic texts, *Sushruta Samhita*.

Medicinal Teas

There is nothing like a nice cup of tea. It soothes us when we are stressed and we indulge in tea drinking as a social activity, as a ritual we share with others.

Tea drinking has been a cultural and social activity for thousands of years. It is believed that it began in ancient times in some Asian cultures as a therapeutic medium and later it formed a part of religious and cultural rituals.

Today we enjoy tea in a multitude of forms and we have revived many of the ancient recipes so that we can enjoy the therapeutic benefits and the exotic flavours. Even ordinary black tea has medicinal properties such as antioxidants that protect against heart disease and cancer.

Teas made from herbs can act as gentle cleansers or purifiers of toxins. Teas such as calendula, dandelion and chamomile can have a detoxifying and anti-inflammatory affect.

Consuming tea made from the right combination of herbs will help you unwind and reduce sleep problems. Buy the fresh dry herbs, preferably organic, and make up some 50gm jars to use as needed.

Sleepy Time Teas

Following are some excellent sleepy time teas. Choose a herb that suits your constitution.

Tip: Storing the fresh herbs in a glass jar in the fridge will keep them fresh longer.

Balm mint or lemon balm (Melissa officinalis)

Balm mint has several names – lemon balm, honey plant and Melissa.

- This is an excellent calming herb ideal for nervous people. Balm mint is good for tension and stress related reactions
- It has a relaxing and sedative action and is useful for nervous stomachs. The word 'balm' signifies the soothing and calming nature of this plant

- Drink 1 cup of balm mint tea for sleeplessness or add 1 strong brewed cup into a bath before bedtime:
  - Add 1 teaspoon of dried lemon balm herb per one cup of boiling water
  - Allow the herb to steep for 5-10 minutes and keep covered in tea pot
  - Strain and drink

Chamomile (Matricaria chamomilla)

The ancient Egyptians were fairly savvy when it came to medicine. Remains of surgical instruments have been found in tombs, and their records show that they understood the benefit of herbs. They actually grew chamomile, a sacred herb, to treat various ailments such as gastrointestinal disorders, women's ailments, liver disorders and kidney stones.

Chamomile is still used today for a variety of conditions including insomnia, flatulence, diarrhoea, stomach complaints, menstrual disorders and toothache as it has sedative, anti-inflammatory and anti-spasmodic properties.

- Infuse one heaped teaspoon of organic chamomile flowers with one cup of boiling water
- Steep for 3-5 minutes and strain
- Drink half an hour before bed
- Soothing alternatives
- Mix chamomile and peppermint as an aid to digestion
- Combine chamomile with lemon grass for relaxing jangled nerves

Caution
Some people can have an allergic reaction to chamomile.

Feverfew (Tanacetum parthenium)

This herb has many benefits including promoting restful sleep, improving digestion, alleviating nausea and vomiting, and for migraines as it has anti-inflammatory, anti-spasmodic and sedative qualities. It also contains nutrients such as vitamins A and C, niacin and iron.

Drinking feverfew tea can help prevent and treat migraines, arthritis, menstrual cramp pain and insomnia.

- Place a teaspoon of dried feverfew herbs in approximately 1 cup of water
- Boil the mixture for 5-10 minutes
- Strain and drink

Hint: Feverfew tea can also be applied to the skin as an insect repellent.

Caution

Avoid feverfew if you are allergic to ragweeds such as daisies, chamomile, chrysanthemums or yarrow. Pregnant women should not use feverfew.

Passionflower (Passiflora incarnata)

The herb passionflower is a native of America, where it was traditionally used as a sedative and calming herb by Native American Indian tribes. It has a sedative effect on people with nervous conditions and it can assist people to achieve a restful sleep.

Its therapeutic qualities can be useful for many purposes including pain relief for toothache and colic, lowering blood pressure, anxiety disorders, nervousness and agitation and as a muscle relaxant.

- Place 1 heaped teaspoon of organic passion flower in one cup of boiling water

- Steep 5 minutes
- Strain and drink half an hour before bed

Caution
Pregnant women should not take passionflower.

Rosemary (Rosmarinus officinalis)

Aromatic rosemary is a native of the Mediterranean region. It gives roast lamb a magnificent aroma and flavour but as a tea it soothes the nerves, relieves insomnia, mental fatigue and headaches. It can also improve mental alertness.

Prior to refrigeration it was used as a preservative for food because it is high in antioxidants. Traditionally, rosemary was employed as an antiseptic and astringent and it is useful for bruising, muscle cramps, circulation, blood pressure and even haemorrhoids.

- Place 1 teaspoon of dried rosemary leaves in 1 cup of boiling water
- Steep for 5 minutes
- Drink this tea up to three times a day

If you are using fresh rosemary leaves you need to use between 2 and 4.4 ml of liquid extract dose per day.

Caution
Rosemary tea should not be drunk by women who are pregnant or lactating, infants under six months old, people with low iron counts (anemia), epilepsy, ulcerative colitis, or high blood pressure.

St John's wort (Hypericum perforatum)

The ancient Greeks used St John's wort to treat nervous conditions and it has been used successfully for the last two thousand years. The primary function of St John's wort is its sedative action so it is a good tool for the treatment of nervous complaints such as neuralgia, mild to medium depression, neurosis, anxiety, tension, sleeplessness and hysteria.

In addition, St John's wort tea can help relieve pain, especially from spinal injuries and puncture wounds, bruises, sores, skin problems, anaemia, headaches, jaundice and congestion in the chest.

For sleep problems

- ✦ Steep one teaspoon of dried St John's wort leaves and flowering tops in a half cup of water for five minutes
- ✦ Drink two cups a day, one in the morning and one in the evening

Caution

St John's wort may increase sensitivity to sunlight and increase the risk of sunburn. It should not be used with viral inhibitor drugs known as protease inhibitors or blood thinning medication.

Cowslip (Primula veris)*

Cowslip is an excellent sedative for stress related problems and it facilitates restful sleep. It grows in fields and mountainous regions and produces golden-yellow coloured flowers.

This herb has many beneficial effects. The flowers, stem and roots are used for therapeutic purposes and the flowers and leaves are rich in vitamin C, beta-carotene, potassium, calcium, and sodium, which help strengthen the immune system.

It has antioxidant properties, can help lower cholesterol and treat gout, heart disease, arthritis and lung disorders. It is also a soothing sedative and effective herb for treating insomnia in adults and children.

Cowslip tea can strengthen the nervous system and heart, alleviate headaches and assist with anxiety. It would not be used on its

---

*(See pg. 141 for Insomnia-be-gone tea).

own as a tea however it is effective as a part of a herbal mixture. Cowslip is used in the great insomnia-be-gone tea mixtures.

Caution

Cowslip has blood thinning properties so it should not be taken by people taking blood thinning drugs.

Chinese Date-Jujube (Zizyphus spinosa)

This herb is a traditional remedy. It has a mildly sedative effect and is good for relieving all sorts of anxiety symptoms such as insomnia, nervous exhaustion and menopausal night sweats — to name but a few.

- Simmer 3 berries in a cup of boiling water for 15 minutes
- Cover and steep for 5 minutes
- Eat the cooked berries to gain the full benefit
- Drink 45 minutes before bed. If you find it has not been very effective drink it twice a day, in the late afternoon and before bed

Insomnia-be-gone Tea Mixtures

Bitter sweet sleep tea

The following tea recipe is useful for insomnia and nervous disorders:

- Add 1 teaspoon of valerian* herb to a cup of boiling water
- Cover and steep for 5 minutes
- Place 1 tablespoon of Swedish bitters in the tea before drinking
- Drink an hour before bed

---

*(See pg. 173)

Balmy sleep tea
Combine and store

- 50g valerian
- 50g Balm mint
- 30g St John's wort
- 30g Cowslip
- 20g Chamomile
    - ✦ Infuse 1 teaspoon of the mixed herbs with 1 cup of boiling water
    - ✦ Steep for 3-5 minutes and strain
    - ✦ Drink 2-3 cups daily

For nervousness and sleep disorders mix the following concoction:

Jitterbug tea
Combine and store

- 35g Chamomile
- 35g Cowslip
- 35g St John's wort
- 25g Passionflower
    - ✦ Infuse 1 teaspoon of the mixed herbs with 1 cup of boiling water
    - ✦ Steep for 3-5 minutes and strain
    - ✦ Drink 2-3 cups daily

Out like a light tea
Combine and store

- 50g of cowslip
- 25g of lavender flowers

- 10g of St. John's wort
- 15g of hop plant
  - ✦ Infuse 1 teaspoon of the mixed herbs with 1 cup of boiling water
  - ✦ Steep for 3 minutes and strain
  - ✦ Drink 2-3 cups daily

Dancing feet tea

This tea is useful for quelling restless leg syndrome.

Combine and store

- 50g yarrow
- 50g peppermint
- 10g oat straw
  - ✦ Infuse 1 heaped teaspoon of the mixed herbs with one cup of boiling water
  - ✦ Steep for 5 minutes
  - ✦ Strain
  - ✦ Drink 1 cup half an hour before bedtime

  Also take 1 valerian capsule.

You can build up to 2-3 cups per day if this tea suits you. However, take the valerian capsule only with the bedtime cup.

Traditional Chinese Medicine Approach (TCM)

Understanding the TCM Approach

Chinese medicine, which has been practiced for more than 3,000 years, places great emphasis on the importance of the rhythms of life.

According to Chinese medicine, regular patterns and rhythms promote good health whereas the opposite leads to disharmony and disease among the organs. Insomnia disrupts these rhythms.

A person needs to adjust to the seasons, weather, political and societal changes to maintain balance in all activities. Sleep is nature's tonic as it eliminates fatigue, compensates for daily wear and tear and restores digestion.

It is believed that during the night, every two hours every organ maximises its efficiency. So during that time if you find that you are waking at a certain time of the night it may be due to an inefficiency or over-stimulation of that organ.

In Chinese medicine when people wake between 2-4 am this is liver organ time. Supporting a healthy liver will aid the function of the whole body, including sleep.

Analysing Your State of Health

Chinese medicine is based on the investigation and analysis of clinical patterns. Imbalances are determined by how the person feels, the tone of the pulse, the look of the tongue and the colour of the skin.

Good health in Chinese medicine means:

+ Your tongue is a pinkish colour with a thin white coating and normal texture
+ The pulse beats five times per breath and at a consistent even rate, rhythm and strength
+ The person experiences no pain or discomfort, has a robust physical build, is spirited, has a good appetite, sleeps well and does a reasonable amount of exercise

Symptoms that are at variance with these factors are considered disease or 'clinical patterns', which are reactions to disease.

A TCM practitioner will deal with these symptoms or clinical patterns with tools such as herbs, food therapy, acupuncture, cupping, Tuina (therapeutic massage) and Moxibustion (Mugwort, used to warm an area).

The philosophy of Chinese medicine is one of prevention and education. The belief is that it is better to lock the stable door before the horse bolts. The Chinese believe in teaching the patient to address their own lifestyle issues of nutrition, diet, exercise, rest, relaxation, stress and environment.

The human being is not separate from the elements of nature that surround him or her. A diagnosis describes the body in terms of the elements; wind, heat, cold, dryness and dampness and the terms yin and yang describe the interdependence and relationship of opposites that make up the whole.

Simply described, yin, the female or cold force, refers to the tissue of the organ and yang, the male or hot force, refers to its function or activity.

Most important is the qi (chi), the life force. This flows through the body along pathways described as meridians. The meridians flow along the surface of the body and through the organs. If one of these becomes blocked then illness occurs. When the qi is flowing freely then the organs can support each other harmoniously. Meridians can be understood as subtle energy pathways that travel throughout our body.

Consider the scenario of a person who goes to a doctor with stomach ulcers. Medication may give some relief but can cause constipation as a side effect. Laxatives may then be taken and then the person's immune system is weakened further and they could develop bronchitis.

Antibiotics are a medication used to treat conditions such as bronchitis. These can cause the side effects of thrush and/or a urinary tract infection. If the bronchitis does not clear, an extra course of antibiotics may be needed, which can cause stress on the liver, leaving the person feeling congested and in pain. So from constipation the person has developed a host of other problems- bronchitis, secondary infections, candida and consequently these cause difficulty in sleeping. It is a slippery slope.

A Chinese medicine practitioner will treat the original imbalance in the digestive system that led to a deficiency in related organs including the intestine, lungs and kidneys, as well as repairing the problems caused by the medication with herbs, acupuncture and diet.

Western medicine can usually only detect illness or disease when it can be quantified through medical tests for example, at a cellular level. Often, prior to any quantifiable symptoms, a person will know that they do not feel quite right. At this stage the cause or problem may not be detectable by pathological tests.

Chinese medicine does not treat the disease name. There is not a standard treatment for people with cancer, sleeplessness or premenstrual tension. Five different people with migraine may have five different reasons for the migraine such as structural, hormonal or stress factors, and those causes will be treated. Someone with a red tongue may have too much heat (yang) and someone with a pale tongue may have internal cold (yin). Chinese medicine treats the clinical patterns.

The TCM way is to maintain balance within the body. If the body and mind are in balance then good health will be restored.

Chinese medicine takes a different approach to insomnia compared to western medicine. The western medical paradigm sees that a person is unable to sleep well, which is usually attributed to some kind of stress, whereas Chinese medicine sees insomnia as a symptom of deficiency or excess. In other words, there is an imbalance or dysfunction in our fundamental substances such as blood, qi, yin and yang or of the major organ systems-heart, lungs, liver, kidneys, spleen.

According to TCM, a person suffering from insomnia usually has an imbalance in the heart and liver. Each of these two organs houses a specific aspect of the spirit. If they are out of balance, they will not be able to house the spirit properly, and the spirit will wander.

A wandering spirit, or 'Shen' disturbance, can manifest in a number of ways, including mood disorders, heart palpitations and most commonly insomnia.

Organ Recital

According to TCM, each organ of the body works throughout the night to both regenerate and carry its normal functions.

Chinese medicine describes several types of insomnia, with each having different origins.

1. *Dreams*

Constant dreams and nightmares can be related to a bladder and gallbladder meridian disorder. Where people cannot stop thinking or have repetitive dreams it is generally considered to be due to a spleen/heart imbalance.

2. *Laying awake*

Having difficulty falling asleep is usually related to an excess condition of the liver or liver and gall bladder.

3. *Waking throughout the night*

It may be easy to fall asleep however, waking throughout the night with difficulty going back to sleep may be due to a deficiency pattern of the heart/spleen.

4. *Waking at the same time each night*

TCM theory says that the body's energy (qi) circulates through the 12 principal meridians (energy pathways) over a 24 hour period. Each meridian relates to an internal organ. If a person wakes or has some unusual symptoms at the same time every day, it is probable that there is an imbalance in the organ system that is problematic at that time.

Chinese Remedies

Many other indications are taken into account when diagnosing a sleep disorder. Treatments will depend on the individual's imbalances and the medicine will be tailored to that. A combination of herbs may be prescribed as well as acupuncture, which can be a very effective treatment.

If you have ever attended a Chinese doctor and taken the herbs that you take home and decoct or brew, you will know that they taste fairly unpleasant; however, it is worth persevering as it is a very effective medicine. Some practitioners use pill forms that are more palatable but often these are not as strong as the herbs.

If this seems like an approach that would suit you, find a qualified Chinese medicine practitioner to work with.

Sleep Tips Oriental Style

- ✦ Ancient Chinese texts state that the position of the body during sleep is important. Sleep curled up on your side and straighten when waking up is the recommended sleep position
- ✦ First make the mind sleep and then the eyes sleep
- ✦ Aid sleep by washing both feet in a basin of hot water. This is believed to draw the blood from the head to the feet. It works by creating healthy circulation and grounds you as

it draws energy away from the head. So, it is helpful and relaxing for someone who thinks a lot
+ Direction of the bed is also important. Chinese medicine philosophy says that the bed head should face in an eastern direction during spring and summer to nourish the yang and west in autumn and winter to nourish the yin. Changing your bed direction will harmonise and nourish the qi

Ayurveda

Fatigue is the great enemy.

– Maharishi Mahesh Yogi

The Ayurvedic Approach

Ayurvedic medicine is believed to be the oldest health care system in the world and was a precursor to modern medicine and natural therapies. Treatments range from lifestyle management to deep therapeutic medicine.

Maharishi Mahesh Yogi was a Vedic scholar who brought 'transcendental meditation' to the west more than 40 years ago. He re-established and restored ayurveda to its ancient completeness which was lost centuries ago due to foreign occupation of India. This approach is usually referred to as Maharishi Ayurveda.

It is considered that treatments are successful because the whole person is attended to. In ayurveda, the term used for health is Swasta. 'Swa' means the 'self' (as in 'swami' or teacher – literally, 'one who leads you to the self.') 'Sta' means to stand (as in statue or stable). Therefore, Swasta means 'to be established in the self'.

Diagnosis is carried out through the pulse, which is said to reflect all patterns of balance and imbalance in the body, mind, emotions and consciousness.

The Three Doshas

The controlling principles of the laws of nature are called the 'doshas.' Doshas are about our biology, psychology and spirit. The three main doshas or principles are vata, pitta and kapha. These elements combine in different permutations in each individual. For good health all three doshas need to be balanced. Imbalances are addressed through diet, herbs, aromatherapy, exercise, meditation and lifestyle.

The three main principles have a great deal of depth. Following is an overview of their characteristics:

Vata is related to change, physical and mental activity, physical movement, excitement, circulation and the intestines and colon. When vata is balanced, it is expressed in intelligence, enthusiasm, quickness, lightness, humour and balanced function of neurophysiology. Vata out of balance can lead to anxiety, tiredness, constipation, pain, insomnia, joint problems, forgetfulness, and disordered functioning in physiological systems.

Pitta is related to energy metabolism, heat, drive, emotion, inner and outer vision, digestion, function of eyes, skin and heart. When balanced it manifests as clear intellect, accurate speech, insight, initiative and command. Out of balance, pitta can cause irritability, impatience, poor digestion, diarrhoea and disorders related to heat including eye and skin disorders.

Kapha is about processing matter and the material structure of the body. Balanced it means stability, calm, balance and strength. Out of balance there could be dullness, lethargy, depression, jealousy, over attachment, respiratory disorders and mucous conditions.

You are What You Digest

'Ojas' is the finest product of digestion that provides energy, enthusiasm, happiness, clarity of thinking, better coordination between the heart and mind, and immunity. The ayurvedic approach aims to create more ojas.

The deepest, most restful sleep is the time when ojas is created and thus, we have enhanced capacity for mental and physical work the next day.

Conversely what we do not want to produce is 'ama'. Ama is produced when your digestive tract is weakened and has to cope with poor food. It is a sticky waste product that is toxic and builds up in the digestive tract. If this continues it can be absorbed back into the body to circulate and settle in places to cause disease.

Ama can clog up circulation channels and restrict the flow of nutrients to cells and organs or obstruct the channels that carry waste from the cells and tissues, resulting in a toxic buildup.

The following symptoms could be due to the build up of ama:

+ A heavy feeling in your body and stiff joints
+ An unpleasant body odour
+ Tongue is coated on waking in the morning
+ Feeling dull and sleepy after eating
+ Difficulty thinking clearly or fogginess in your mind
+ Symptoms also include diarrhoea, constipation, joint pains, sadness, dullness, lowered immunity, frequently catching colds and flu

A body clogged up with disease generating ama is going to struggle with normal functioning and cause the doshas to be out of balance and when the doshas are out of balance, we may have trouble getting to sleep.

To solve any kind of health issue, including sleep disorders, a practitioner will recommend herbal remedies in conjunction with lifestyle and dietary adjustments. Food is medicine and culinary herbs and spices can also have a therapeutic effect. Understanding their value means that you can create food that will enhance the way you are feeling.

According to ayurveda, six tastes should all be present in a balanced meal. These are sweet, salty, sour, bitter, pungent and astringent. The presence of these tastes in a meal can help counteract imbalances in the doshas.

Sleep Disorders According to Ayurveda

1. Difficulty falling asleep

Those who toss and turn with a busy mind may have a vata imbalance due to stress and anxiety.

Solution

- Eat more sweet, sour and salty foods
- Eat three warm, cooked meals that is, breakfast, lunch and dinner, at the same time every day
- Get to bed before 10 pm and get up by 6 am because regular sleep times help regulate sleep patterns
- Avoid rushing, be it for work or any other activity as this causes stress
- Gandharva Veda music is wonderfully therapeutic; play it before bed time for a good night's sleep

2. Intermittent waking

This is where you fall asleep but wake up every 90 minutes with a racing heart, tense muscles and feel fear, anger and sadness. Another related pattern is waking up between 2 am and 4 am feeling wide awake, full of energy and unable to fall back to sleep.

This can happen if there is a pitta imbalance or because of emotional trauma.

Solution

- ✦ Avoid spicy foods
- ✦ Eat more sweet, bitter and astringent tasting foods
- ✦ Eat regularly and do not miss out on meals
- ✦ Eat enough dinner so you do not wake up feeling hungry

3. Sleep long hours and wake up falling unrefreshed

This can take the form of waking in the early morning hours or having long sleep ins. Whatever the situation, you will feel tired, sluggish and exhausted even though you have had a full night's sleep.

Solution

- ✦ Get up before 6 am
- ✦ Do a morning self body massage with curd, warm sesame oil*. Sesame oil is rich in antioxidants and nourishes the skin and leaves you feeling soft and relaxed
- ✦ Exercise daily
- ✦ Sip warm water throughout the day
- ✦ Avoid eating too much heavy, sweet, sour and salty foods
- ✦ Eat a light, warm dinner such as soup and season food with fresh ginger and a small amount of black pepper

No matter which kind of imbalance you have, it is recommended that you fall asleep before 10 pm to achieve a more restful sleep. The quality of your sleep will be deeper and falling asleep will not be difficult.

---

*Sesame oil needs to be warmed before use. Just place it in a bowl of hot water or on the stove in boiling water until it is warmed.

Herbal Bliss

A practitioner will prescribe herbs such as musk root and Indian valerian, which are pro-sedative, meaning that they help the person relax into sleep. A large number of research studies show that Indian valerian induces sleep. Herbs such as brahmi and ashwagandha, restore the body's own inner intelligence to improve the quality of sleep. Any damage that has resulted from a lack of sleep such as compromised immunity will also need to be attended to so that more illness does not occur.

The herbs work to improve sleep quality therefore enhancing concentration, reducing stress and increasing a person's ability to cope with whatever the day brings.

Ayurvedic teas, oils and herbs can assist these imbalances but it is preferable to consult an ayurvedic practitioner who will prescribe appropriate treatments.

Naturopathy

The term naturopathy covers a wide range of natural medicine regimes. The modalities employed by naturopaths are homoeopathy, western and Chinese herbalism, massage, herbal medicine, iridology, nutrition, flower essences and any other modalities that the naturopath may wish to pursue.

Natural therapies sustain and improve health by supporting and regulating natural functions rather than treating the symptoms of disease. For example, where a doctor will prescribe antibiotics to clear up an infection, a herbalist will use plants to stimulate a person's immune system so they will be able to fight an infection.

Prescriptions are individualised to the present patient rather than for a particular condition.

Often natural medicines can do the job of pharmaceuticals and be more effective and long lasting because the whole person is attended to rather than just an isolated ailment or symptom. The treatment encourages the body to heal itself.

A holistic approach can be challenging to the patient because they may have to seriously re-evaluate their lifestyle choices and make real changes. Going down the holistic road means making a commitment to sustained good health and this takes time and effort.

A naturopath will generally consider the mind, body and spirit of the patient when conducting a consultation. An initial session will take around an hour and you will be asked everything from the state of your relationships to emotional difficulties and health concerns. Effective treatment depends on knowing all the fine points of an individual's situation.

For those people who are not so open to discussing these aspects of their lives, this process may seem intrusive and difficult, but a good practitioner will be sensitive and draw out the information slowly and gently if necessary.

A skilled naturopath can create a functional assessment of the organs and recognise the slow process of deterioration of function, whereas often, western medicine is unable to diagnose disease until it is well advanced. They can establish links between seemingly isolated episodes of illness and assess areas of weakness and predisposition for illness. Like Chinese medicine, a pattern is established and strategies can be put in place to prevent and hopefully reverse the escalation of weaknesses before more serious conditions develop.

Not all naturopaths will use all the modalities that they have been taught. Many prefer to concentrate on using one main modality such as herbal medicine or homoeopathy and use others as adjuncts to those treatments, or in combination.

Practitioners individualise their treatment modes according to their success and talent in certain areas and the needs of the client. For example, a person may not react well to some herbs; they may be too sensitive or allergic and therefore respond better to the vibrational healing of homoeopathy. Many naturopaths say that children respond readily to homoeopathy and it may also be more suitable for kids because the herbs are less palatable.

When it comes to sleep, herbs, supplements and homoeopathic remedies will be recommended depending on the person's picture. They will also recommend lifestyle modification and possibly other adjunct modalities. Following are some of the treatments that are employed by naturopaths:

Vitamins, Minerals, Amino Acids and Insomnia

Thousands of years before humans understood the scientific nature of what we eat and drink, their connectedness with nature gave them insight into what the earth provided to maintain health.

As the world became more 'sophisticated' and industrialisation permeated western life, and as food became scarce to those who lacked money, so did the health of people become eroded.

The more humans controlled their environment, used pesticides on the soils and poisoned, over-worked and depleted them of minerals and nutrients, the more populations became sick.

Up to around 100 years ago, vitamin C deficiency called scurvy, generally suffered by sailors, was still a common occurrence. This deficiency diminished the ability to heal wounds, caused bleeding gums and ultimately death.

Other nasty diseases such as beriberi, caused by a lack of vitamin B, and rickets, caused by a deficiency of vitamin D, were still common 60 years ago. Rickets led to weakened bones that would facture easily. A myriad of other disorders developed because of a lack of vitamins and minerals.

Minerals and vitamins are the body's construction and maintenance materials. Without them in the right balance we will not grow, develop and stay healthy. Minerals are inorganic compounds and they are not as volatile as vitamins as they are not destroyed as easily by heat or poor handling. They are essential to many functions including the organs and they help to regulate body processes.

Our bodies store over 60 minerals; 22 of those are vital for maintaining health.

Deficiencies in certain vitamins, minerals, amino acids and enzymes such as calcium, magnesium, B vitamins, folic acid and melatonin, can disrupt sleep. A balanced diet, properly prepared and digested will fill your body with all the right fuel.

Vitamins that Aid Sleep

A good tool in the arsenal to fight and defeat insomnia is the B group of vitamins as they have a sedative effect on the nerves. The B vitamins are involved in the metabolism of neurotransmitters such as serotonin, which aids in the regulation of sleep.

The best food sources of B vitamins are liver, whole grains, wheat germ, tuna, walnuts, peanuts, bananas, sunflower seeds and blackstrap molasses.

It is important to note that the most efficient way to take B vitamins is as a complex, that way you will not experience an imbalance by taking too much of one and not enough of another.

Be guided by your health practitioner to determine whether your sleep problems may be helped by the B vitamins.

B is for Blissful Sleep
Vitamin B3 (Niacin):

Vitamin B3 is otherwise known as niacin. Like other B vitamins, niacin is essential for the manufacture of enzymes that provide cells with energy.

Niacin is involved in over 200 enzyme reactions and is essential for healthy skin, tongue and digestive tract tissues as well as the formation of red blood cells. It is also important for the synthesis of various hormones and the normal functioning of the brain and nervous system. Niacin helps you to relax and fall asleep quicker. It is involved in a lot of important functions such as:

- Sleep regulation
- Protein, fat and carbohydrate metabolisation
- Dilation of arteries to facilitate blood circulation
- Prevention of plaque forming on the walls of arteries
- Symptoms of niacin deficiency include
  - Fatigue
  - Loss of appetite
  - Diarrhoea
  - Irritability
  - Headache, mood swings, loss of memory
  - In advanced cases, a condition called pellagra develops which gives you dermatitis, dementia and diarrhoea

Research conducted on animals who were given large doses of niacinamide showed that they experienced an increase in the amount of time spent in the REM sleep stage.

A wide range of foods contain niacin. It is more abundantly found in animal sources, although a few plant sources are rich in niacin as well.

Niacin foods include:

- Lean red meat
- Fish
- Organ meats such as kidney and liver
- Prawns
- Pork
- Dairy products
- Almonds and seeds
- Wheat products
- Beans, rice bran
- Green leafy vegetables, carrots, turnips and celery
- Nutritional yeast

If a person has a vitamin B3 deficiency and they take tryptophan to assist sleep, the tryptophan will not convert to serotonin, so it is vital to have stable B levels. If there is a deficiency in B3 most of the tryptophan will be used instead to convert to vitamin B3.

Vitamin B6 (Pyridoxine)

Taking vitamin B6 daily can help prevent insomnia because it assists in the production of the neurotransmitters-serotonin and dopamine.

It will be 'steady as she goes' because this vitamin affects the equilibrium of our mood and assists with cravings for sweets, which can interfere with sleep because blood sugar levels are affected.

A B6 deficiency can lead to or aggravate the effects of PMS as it is involved in balancing female hormonal fluctuation, mood and behaviour, fluid retention due to PMS, mood swings and depression.

Foods that provide B6:

- Seafood
- Silver beet
- Capsicums
- Turnip greens
- Broccoli
- Cauliflower
- Pork
- Beef
- Chicken
- Turkey
- Whole grains
- Wheatgerm
- Sunflower seeds
- Pistachio nuts

The combination of vitamin B6, niacin and folic acid are sometimes used to treat insomnia. Increasing the intake of these vitamins is likely to be effective in cases of deficiency.

Caution

Vitamin B6 is one of the few vitamins that have the potential to cause toxic side effects if it is taken in doses above 2 mg per day. Only take it in consultation with your physician. Another contraindication is for people with Parkinson's disease who are taking L-dopa treatment as it can reduce the effectiveness of the drug.

Vitamin B7 (Biotin)

Biotin is a water soluble B vitamin that enhances the quality of REM sleep. It is also involved in the following functions:
- Metabolism of carbohydrate, amino acids and protein
- Maintenance of immune system
- Release of energy from food
- Production of fatty acids and glucose
- Cell and hair growth
- Function of several enzymes

Food sources that contain biotin:
- Royal jelly
- Kidney
- Liver
- Brewer's yeast
- Egg yolk
- Fish
- Nuts
- Oatmeal
- Beans
- Milk, cheese, yoghurt and egg whites
- Rice
- Beef and liver
- Salmon
- Wheatgerm
- Whole meal bread
- Sunflower seeds

- Mushrooms
- Broccoli

Symptoms of a biotin deficiency include sleeplessness, hair loss, lethargy, depression and facial rash.

An adequate intake of biotin is around 30 mg per day and it should be taken daily if appropriate.

Vitamin B9 (Folate)

The name folate or folic acid, suggests foliage, and it is leafy green vegetables that are the best sources of it as well as fortified grains and legumes.

Folate plays a critical role in many biological processes. It participates in the methylation pathway. This is a special transport system where food delivers folate in a form that is combined with amino acids into the liver and other cells. Folate plays an important role in cell division and growth and without adequate amounts of folate, cells cannot divide properly. These aspects can lead to a range of symptoms that relate to insomnia.

A folate deficiency is common as many drugs impair your body's ability to absorb or metabolise folate. These include antacids, H2 blockers for acid reflux, diabetes medication, non-specific anti-inflammatory drugs and the oral contraceptive pill.

Deficiency can cause symptoms such as confusion, forgetfulness, irritability, mood changes, tiredness and insomnia.

Foods that contain B9:

- Nuts and seeds
- Sprouts
- Organ meats including liver
- Grains
- Poultry

✦ Oranges and grapefruits
✦ Green leafy vegetables

It is recommended that women take folate prior to and during pregnancy to prevent a range of neural tube birth defects including spina bifida, as well as heart and palate defects. A folate deficiency can also cause anaemia.

Vitamin B12 (Cobalamin)

Vitamin B12 is stored in the liver. A deficiency causes damage to the nervous system. It helps metabolize fats and carbohydrates, synthesise proteins and grow and replicate cells. B12 is required for the normal activity of nerve cells and works with folate and B6 in the methylation cycle.

However, it is mostly known for treating anaemia and pernicious anaemia. In fact anaemia and feelings of exhaustion are usually the first signs of B12 deficiency.

Studies have also shown that it is an effective anti-insomnia vitamin that enhances sleep quality.

In severe cases, vitamin B12 injections can be used to treat insomnia. A doctor will administer injections if it is appropriate.

Good food sources of B12:

✦ Seafood
✦ Eggs
✦ Dairy products
✦ Brewers' yeast
✦ Turkey
✦ Veal
✦ Lamb

Minerals are a Mine of Good Health

Because of the depletion of minerals in our soils, our food does not provide sufficient essential minerals and this is one factor that is seriously compromising our health. The following minerals affect our ability to sleep:

Magnesium

Magnesium is involved in around 300 bodily functions and its lack can cause a myriad of symptoms including nervousness and sleeplessness.

- Magnesium supplements have a muscle relaxing effect, which may be beneficial for sleep if they are taken at night
- It is best to take a mixture of magnesium and calcium 45 minutes before bedtime for a tranquilising effect. Be guided by your health practitioner because the mineral balance is important. Taking too much may impede absorption of another mineral.
- Magnesium rich foods include:
  - Kelp
  - Wheat bran
  - Almonds
  - Brazil nuts, cashews, walnuts
  - Blackstrap molasses
  - Brewer's yeast
  - Red meat
  - Turkey, chicken
  - Sunflower seeds, sesame seeds
  - Dark chocolate
  - Legumes
  - Spinach
  - Banana

Iron

Iron deficiencies can exacerbate sleeping difficulties. It is also a helpful mineral for restless leg syndrome. Studies suggest that restless leg syndrome caused by iron deficiency is relatively common in the elderly

- Iron supplements can be taken but they should be combined with vitamin C because vitamin C helps the body absorb the iron more efficiently
- Juicing spinach and parsley provides a great source of iron and can help reduce the symptoms of restless leg syndrome

Tip: Avoid drinking tea whilst eating meat because both caffeine and tannin decrease the absorption of iron in the blood. It is wise to drink tea or coffee at least half an hour after eating meat.

Caution

Iron supplements should not be taken unless blood tests show you are genuinely deficient. Because it is a very oxidising mineral, it can exacerbate any inflammatory condition.

Calcium

We know how important the mineral calcium is for strong bones and teeth and the dire consequence of a lack of it is osteoporosis. Bones and teeth consume 99 per cent of the body's calcium. The other one per cent is used for other bodily functions including muscle contraction, the expansion and contractions of blood vessels, hormone secretions and transmitting impulses throughout the nervous system.

People whose diets are poor, who drink excessive carbonated, sweet fizzy drinks and eat a lot of processed foods may be in need of calcium.

Calcium deficiency causes:

- Insomnia
- Depression
- Nerve sensitivity
- Muscle twitching
- Brittle nails
- Irritability
- Palpitations
- Muscle spasms and cramps
- Numbness
- Stiffness

Good sources of calcium:

Calcium from milk and milk products are absorbed more easily than calcium from most vegetables, with the exception of dark green leafy vegetables such as kale, broccoli, turnip and mustard greens.

- Kale
- Kelp
- Tofu
- Canned fish with bones
- Walnuts
- Sunflower
- Seeds
- Broccoli
- Cauliflower
- Soybeans

Note: A 1990 study published in the **American Journal of Clinical Nutrition** showed that more calcium is absorbed from kale than milk.

Taking calcium supplements can cause constipation. Taking it with magnesium helps prevent that. Those who are constipated from taking calcium need to eat extra fiber and make sure they are well hydrated.

Calcium deficiency causes people to be restless and wakeful in bed. As a mixture, calcium and magnesium produce a calming effect. A lack of calcium and magnesium can cause leg cramps at night.

- Ingesting calcium from food has more of a sedative effect on the body than supplements
- Adults need doses of approximately 600 milligrams of calcium to achieve a relaxing effect. It is generally taken in tablet form. The dose for people over 50 years old and suspected of having osteoporosis is 1,500-2,000 mg daily in divided doses, after meals and at bedtime

Building Blocks

Just like with vitamins and minerals, you cannot live without amino acids. Approximately 75 per cent of our body is made up of them and they are essential to nearly every bodily function and chemical reaction.

Without amino acids our body cannot manufacture protein because proteins are made from chains of amino acids. Water is the largest constituent of our body and protein is the second largest constituent so we are in big trouble without them.

The following amino acids are vital to the sleep process.

The Chain Gang

There are three main types of amino acids – essential, non-essential and semi-essential. The essential ones must be included in our diet every day because our body cannot manufacture them. They make up a large proportion of our vital body bits such as muscles, tendons, organs, glands, nails and hair. Cell repair, maintenance and growth depend on them.

Considering that one of the essential amino acids is tryptophan, a deficiency in amino acids can interrupt sleep.

Meat, fish, eggs, milk and soya beans contain all the essential amino acids.

Tripping off to Sleep

Tryptophan (L-tryptophan) is an amino acid that plays a key role in the repair of protein tissues and in creating new protein. As you will know by now tryptophan is converted into serotonin, the sleep inducing chemical. It also enhances the brains ability to produce melatonin, the hormone that regulates the body clock.

Tryptophan supplementation is more effective for those who have sleep onset insomnia (that means having trouble falling asleep), since its greatest effect is to shorten the time taken to get to sleep. It has been found to improve the time taken to go from a wakeful to a sleeping state as well as increasing the time spent in stage 4 sleep, which is the deep sleep stage.

Doses of approximately 2 grams (depending on the individual) of tryptophan taken with vitamin B3, B6, zinc and magnesium at bedtime have also been found to improve severe sleep apnoea. To be effective it needs to be taken in relatively high doses; doses less than 2,000 mg are generally not effective.

Foods that contain tryptophan are milk, turkey, soya beans, red meat, chicken, tuna, salmon, shrimp, cod, halibut, nuts, seeds, legumes, spinach, mustard greens and asparagus.

It is most effective to eat a complex carbohydrate with tryptophan for improved absorption. It may take one hour for the tryptophan in food to reach the brain so this needs to be taken into consideration in the night time routine.

Note: Many naturopaths who use bio-resonance machines such as the Mora machine can ascertain which amino acids are necessary for the individual and can offer tryptophan as a vibrational medicine, which is similar to a homoeopathic medicine.

Wakey Wakey

Phosphatidylserine is a word that is very hard to pronounce. It is also an amino acid that helps the brain regulate the amount of cortisol produced by the adrenal glands. Cortisol is usually at high levels in the morning to assist us to wake up. Otherwise levels of cortisol rise when we are stressed so people who suffer with a lot of stress at night may not be able to sleep because of these increased levels.

Phosphatidylserine is an essential component in all of our cells, specifically the cell membrane. It is especially important in maintaining the structure of cells and it is therefore involved in moving important nutrients into them and pumping out the waste products. Our bodies make all the phosphatidylserine we need. However, for a therapeutic dose we need supplementation.

Sleep Lag

During the day, the pineal gland produces the neurotransmitter serotonin. However, at night, it stops producing serotonin and makes melatonin, the hormone that triggers sleep. The production of melatonin varies according to the amount of light you are exposed to. Levels should be high at night and low in the morning, and cortisol should be low at night and high in the morning. A lack of sleep and lack of exposure to darkness may suppress the natural production of melatonin.

Taken as a supplement, melatonin is said to induce sleep without any negative side effects and it is very useful for people who have disruptions to their sleep/wake cycle such as shift workers or people with jet lag. Melatonin helps to reset the body clock and place you back into the right time zone. It is even a powerful antioxidant.

It is believed that melatonin levels decline with age, which is one reason why older people can experience sleep problems.

Melatonin Research

In a 1997[*] placebo controlled double blind cross over study, the effects of melatonin were studied by researchers. After sleeping seven hours in the night, eight men were given either a placebo or doses of melatonin at 10 am.

Results

- Those who took melatonin fell asleep in a significantly reduced time
- The melatonin significantly increased the total amount of sleep and decreased the amount of times they woke up after they had gone to sleep

Other studies have shown that when melatonin is used for jet lag the symptoms are decreased and normal energy levels return sooner.

There's a lot of evidence that our serotonin levels are compromised due to negative lifestyle factors. No surprises there when you consider the amount of stress that people are under.

A melatonin deficit can cause:

- Sleeplessness
- Sugar cravings
- Weight gain
- Depression
- Aches and pains

---

[*]Hughes RJ, Badia P, Sleep promoting and hypothermic effects of daytime melatonin administration in humans. Sleep, 1997 February, 20.2, 124-31.

- All kinds of headaches
- Narcolepsy
- Fibromyalgia, and the list goes on

Boosting the melatonin levels for a period can assist with resetting the body clock so that the body's cycle is restored and melatonin production can begin in full flight again. It can also improve the quality and duration of sleep where the cycle is disrupted. But do not forget to attend to your lifestyle issues and health at the same time.

It is common for elderly people to have reduced levels of melatonin so it can be an effective treatment for them.

Get tested

Melatonin and cortisol levels can be determined by functional pathology tests such as salivary hormone tests. This will tell you whether it is appropriate to use melatonin as a sleep treatment. Naturopaths and doctors can request these tests.

For optimum effect your doctor or natural therapist should prescribe this treatment, however, if you think melatonin is suitable for you, start with 1.5 mg daily taken 2 hours before bedtime. If this is not effective, gradually increase the dosage until an effective level is reached. Do not take more than 5 mg daily.

Melatonin can cause drowsiness if taken during the day. If morning drowsiness is experienced after taking melatonin at night, reduce the dosage. In some cases of depression, daytime doses of melatonin can increase depression.

Caution

Do not take melatonin if you are pregnant, have cancer of the blood or immune system or kidney disease.

Melatonin may also be contraindicated for those with autoimmune disorders and immune system cancers such as lymphoma and leukaemia. Because melatonin suppresses corticosteroid activity, those who are taking corticosteroids for anti-inflammatory or immune suppressive purposes, such as transplant patients should exercise caution with melatonin supplementation. Melatonin could also interfere with fertility. It is also contraindicated during pregnancy and lactation.

Treatment for RLS Caused by Deficiencies

Restless leg syndrome is also linked to deficiencies in some minerals.

Iron
An iron deficiency can cause RLS because iron is vital for the production of the chemical dopamine. A dopamine deficiency can cause disturbances in the body's movements. A simple blood test can be taken to determine iron level.

According to the extent of the deficiency, a person can either increase their iron intake by eating iron rich foods or take an iron supplement*.

Folic acid
A folic acid deficiency has also been associated with RLS, so folic acid supplements can also assist.

Vitamin E
Circulation and the supply of oxygen to tissues and nerves can be improved by taking Vitamin E, so this can be useful in the treatment of restless legs syndrome.

Magnesium
Magnesium is a mineral that can help with muscle spasms, which give rise to RLS.

Calcium

Calcium plays a vital role in proper nerve function and muscle contraction. Lack of calcium can cause muscle spasms, which is also a symptom of RLS.

Because there are a number of possible causes of RLS it is important to consult a health practitioner who will determine what your deficiencies are and advise about the appropriate supplement to suit your physiology.

Some prescription drugs can cause RLS. If this is the case you may need to stop or change the medication under the supervision of your doctor. This will usually relieve the symptoms.

Herbal Medicines, Supplements and Insomnia

Like any medicine, herbs should be prescribed by a qualified professional. As you will read many herbs can assist people to sleep, however not all are suitable for everyone. Also herbs are powerful medicines and have the ability to interact with prescription medicines.

Herbs and Insomnia

This section explains how herbs can help sleep issues.

Valerian (Valeriana officinalis)

Valerian, a native of Europe and North America, is commonly used to induce sleep. It has a long tradition of use as a sedative and tranquilliser. The part of the plant that is used is the root and rhizome.

Valerian is used mainly for the treatment of insomnia. It decreases the time it takes to go to sleep and improves the quality and length of sleep.

Properties include:

- Anxiety relief
- Lowers blood pressure
- Enhances the flow of bile
- Relaxes intestinal and other smooth muscles

Valerian can be used in a number of forms including teas, liquid extracts and tinctures.

Caution

Valerian may cause a sensation of heavy headedness and morning sleepiness in some people. In rare cases it can cause stimulation.

Hops (Humulus lupulus)

We most commonly know Hops as an ingredient in beer. Historically hops have been used for everything from boils, bruises, cramps and coughs to cystitis, delirium, diarrhoea, dyspepsia, fever, fits, hysteria and inflammation. The Delaware Indians heated a small bag of leaves to apply to earache or toothache and they used it as a sedative. They drank Hop tea several times a day to alleviate nervousness. The plant part used is the leafy cone shaped strobile flower.

Properties include:

- Anti-spasmodic, making it a strong digestive aid
- Soporific and sedative
- Muscle relaxant

Caution

There is a belief that Hops should not be used if a person is suffering from depression.

Skullcap (Scutellaria laterifolia)

Some other names that Skullcap is known by are helmet flower, blue pimpernel, quaker bonnet.

Skullcap is a powerful perennial herb with cap-like flowers. It grows in North America and is cultivated in Europe. It has many applications; one being as a herb that calms people who suffer from nervous disorders. The leaves and flowers are used for insomnia.

It is a useful treatment for a wide range of conditions including epilepsy, insomnia, hysteria, anxiety, restless leg syndrome, cramping, delirium tremens and withdrawal from tranquillisers. and barbiturates to name a few.

Properties include:

- Anti-inflammatory
- Anti-spasmodic
- Fever reduction
- Nervine (soothes the nervous system)
- Sedative
- Anxiety
- Anti-depressant
- Sleep inducing

A good insomnia remedy and nervous system tonic is a combination of skullcap, wild lettuce and passion flower. Or a sachet can be filled with skullcap leaves and placed under the pillow when going to sleep.

Otherwise it comes in a number of forms such as tinctures and powders, however, it is best to have it prescribed.

Caution

Skullcap should not be taken by diabetics or pregnant women as it can induce miscarriage. Overdosing can cause giddiness, stupor, confusion and twitching. Do not use it if you are taking anti-histamines or sedative medications as it intensifies the effects on the central nervous system.

Zizyphus (spiny jujube or sour Chinese date seed)

Zizyphus spinosa is a commonly used herb in TCM practice, and has been employed in western herbal medicine to treat anxiety and insomnia.

Properties include:

- Hypnotic (sleep inducing)
- Sedative
- Hypotensive (lowers blood pressure)
- Releases excessive sweating
- Reduces hot flushes

It is traditionally used to nourish the liver and heart and calm the spirit in cases of sleep that is disturbed by dreams as well as insomnia, irritability, palpations with anxiety, excessive sweating and night sweats.

Passion flower (Passiflora incarnata)

The flowering and fruiting tops of passion flower have been used traditionally as herbal remedies for nervousness, restlessness, wakefulness, hysteria and insomnia.

Properties include:

- Anxiety
- Prevent spasms

- Sedative
- Hypnotic
- Insomnia
- Restlessness
- Irritability
- Nervous headache

Caution

There are no known contraindications. However, passion flowers safety has not been established for pregnant or nursing mothers. So, it is best to avoid using it in these circumstances.

Kava kava (Piper methysticum)

Kava is renowned as a recreational herb that is used in the Pacific Islands during celebrations. It causes drinkers to feel calm, relaxed and sociable. Taken in large doses it can induce sleep so it can be an effective treatment for insomnia, restlessness and anxiety.

The active properties of Kava are believed to act as a central nervous system depressant.

Properties include:

- Anxiety
- Hypnotic
- Analgesic

Caution

Kava should not be taken by those suffering from Parkinson's disease, especially in the case of elderly people. Kava should also be avoided for those people on benzodiazepines and antipsychotic drugs. There are also safety concerns for long term use, including liver damage and it can sometimes cause a rash. If this happens, discontinue its use.

St John's wort (Hypericum perforatum)

The ancient Greeks were switched onto St John's wort because it was useful for treating nervous conditions. A couple of thousand years later it is still a popular herbal remedy for use in cases of mild to medium depression. In addition it has sedative and pain-relieving qualities that help improve the quality of sleep.

Hypericin is the active constituent that elevates mood. It is believed that hypericum enhances serotonin, norepinephrine and dopamine which have anti-depressant and anti-anxiety effects. And some initial research suggests that it also lowers cortisol levels.

St John's wort can be taken as a liquid extract, in tablet form or as a tea.

Caution

Although, St John's wort has a long history of safe use there are a number of contraindications. Do not use St John's wort if you are taking anti-depressants, the oral contraceptive pill, are pregnant or lactating. Recent reports suggest it may interfere with medications given during organ transplant. It can also react with foods and drinks containing tyramine such as red wine, cheese, beer, yeast and pickled herring. St. John's wort makes the skin more light sensitive so take care when exposing yourself to the sun.

Gotukolaor Indian pennywort (Centella asiatica)

This is an ayurvedic herb that has sedative properties and helps improve memory and mental function, plus it is useful for people who cannot relax. It also encourages the production of neurotransmitters, so it can improve brain function.

Gotukola is also used for many other conditions such as relieving congestion from colds, reducing fever and skin conditions.

It contains chemicals called triterpines (saponins), which enhance the formulation of collagen in bones, cartilage and connective tissue so they promote healthy blood vessels by strengthening their walls and improving blood flow.

It is a plant with a red flower that grows in swampy areas of India, Pakistan, Sri Lanka, South Africa, Australia, China, Madagascar and the southern United States.

Caution
Gotukola should not be used by pregnant or lactating women, or those who are trying to conceive. It can also be toxic when used in high doses.

Wild lettuce (Lactucavirosa)

Wild lettuce is another ancient herb, renowned for its tranquillising and pain relieving effects. This herb has a number of aliases including 'lettuce opium' and it is part of the Asteraceae – Aster/Sunflower family. It has properties that can relieve pain and was widely used before the advent of synthetic pain medications.

An opium related substance in wild lettuce makes it a natural sedative to aid sleep and soothe an agitated nervous system. It also contains an anti-cramping agent and is helpful for headaches and muscular and gut pain. Its properties can calm the mind and relieve anxiety and even quell restless leg syndrome.

If you suffer from a sleep disorder make lettuce a part of your dinner or drink lettuce juice.

Caution
People who are allergic to plants in the Asteraceae family should avoid wild lettuce use. It should not be taken with sedatives and drugs with sedative effects including alpha-blockers, beta-block-

ers, anaesthetics, analgesics and tricyclic anti-depressants. Also, taking excessive doses can actually cause insomnia.

Oatstraw (Avena sativa)

Oats, also known as hafer, green oat and groats, are a warming food renowned for lowering cholesterol and being a good source of fiber. The whole plant is action packed with health sustaining goodness. Oats plus the oat straw are rich in calcium, iron, phosphorus, zinc, magnesium, vitamins A, C, E and K, B-complex vitamins, potassium, zinc, magnesium, proteins and silica.

The seeds and the leaves of the oat plant are used medicinally. Oatstraw has the following effects:

- Nervine – it soothes the nervous system, and relieves stress and exhaustion
- Anti-depressant
- Insomnia
- Exhaustion
- Can improve mental function and concentration, and sharpen focus
- It can even enhance the libido
- Nutritive – nourishing to the nervous system

Chamomile (Chamomilla maritima)

As mentioned earlier in the chapter in 'Medicinal teas', chamomile is used popularly as a calming herbal tea. However, it has many other beneficial properties such as:

- Anti-inflammatory
- Anti-allergy
- Digestion aid

- Relieves muscle spasms as it is a relaxant
- Aid for wound healing
- Sleeping difficulties
- Aids relaxation

As a natural remedy, it is used to assist in the treatment of a number of conditions including insomnia, asthma, hay fever, sinusitis, gastrointestinal disturbance, menstrual and menopause problems, nervous tension, tension and digestive headaches.

Chamomile can be taken as a tea or herbal tincture.

Caution

Those who are sensitive to the ragweed family should avoid chamomile.

Herbs for Menopause

One of the earliest indicators that a middle aged woman is heading into the next stage of her life is when her sleep patterns start to change due to hormonal fluctuations. By maintaining hormonal balance, sleep patterns also have the chance to remain regular.

Following are some recommendations that have the possibility of maintaining hormonal balance. Visit your natural therapist or holistic doctor for tailored treatments.

- Naturopathy suggests that menopausal women benefit from eating a diet rich in calcium and phyto-oestrogens, which are found primarily in soy products
- Herbs high in plant oestrogens and progesterone are red clover, wild yam, sage, vitex agnus-castus (Chaste tree) and dong quai (Angelica)
- Sedative remedies such as passion flower (Passiflora incarnata), skull cap and chamomile are helpful for interrupted sleep patterns

- Avoid foods rich in oxalic acids such as spinach and rhubarb because the oxalic acids bind to the body's calcium and impede absorption
- The liver is important to hormone regularity so a healthy liver will assist not only in sleep but also in the level of symptoms for any female function. Herbs that can support liver function are dandelion and milk thistle
- Sage and zizyphus are commonly used to help with hot flushes in menopausal women either as a tea or in herbal tincture

Herbs and Supplements to Help Conquer Premenstrual Symptoms (PMS)

Approximately 150 premenstrual symptoms have been identified. Insomnia, anxiety and nervous tension are some of the most common along with the raging tummy cramps.

Kava kava (Piper methysticum)
Kava is useful for PMS where a woman is suffering from anxiety, restlessness, stress and insomnia.

Lemon balm (Melissa officinalis)
Generally, lemon balm is used as a remedy for nervousness, depression, anxiety and insomnia. So, if these symptoms relate to you during PMS then they will provide relief.

Chaste berry (Vitex agnus-castus)
Vitex has been traditionally used for gynaecological disorders such as PMS and polycystic ovarian syndrome. However, new research has shown that it may be useful for treating sleep disorders. This includes poor sleep maintenance and problems associated with shift work and jet lag.

Cramp bark (Viburnum opulus)
Reduces menstrual cramps as well as acts as a mild sedative.

Flower Essences

People in ancient times were in touch with the fruits of nature as much as most of us have become removed from them in the modern world. They intuitively understood and harnessed healing essences.

The early twentieth century saw a revival of this ancient healing practice with Dr Edward Bach's development of 38 flower essences, which are renowned throughout the world. These remedies provide spiritual and emotional healing. Rescue Remedy is one that is widely used for stress and trauma.

Flower essences, elixirs made from nature's flora, have powerful medicinal qualities. Understanding them and how they interact gives you a useful tool in the sleepy time armoury.

This is How They Work

We are all interconnected with nature. One reason is that we are made from the same substances, so when we view, touch and smell a plant, flower, grass, root, seeds that have begun to shoot, tree bark or a leaf, it will elicit a sensation or emotion.

Such experiences are encoded into our cells and have the ability to affect us deeply on many different levels. An example of this is the rose. It evokes an emotional response because of its beauty and its uplifting and joyous fragrance. The essence of a rose opens our heart energies and boosts our mood. It can also offer courage and peacefulness. We feel the effects as an emotion that touches our heart. There is a reason that men and women have been offering each other roses for centuries as a demonstration of love and affection.

Or consider the oak tree, with its strong, solid, grounded structure. According to Dr Edward Bach, ingesting an essence made from the oak tree assists the 'strong' person who feels invincible. This type of person consequently works and is active constantly without incorporating the balance of relaxation and leisure into their lives.

The problem is that when they become ill it is usually a major issue that stops them in their tracks. They get very sick and cannot continue the pace.

Therefore, the bark of the tree may be appreciated as an element that creates boundary and protection from negative external influences. Essences made from bark will be used as a protective device or as a filter for negativity.

Every element of a plant – the flower, root, bark, seed, shoot and leaf is significant and each species of a flowering plant and tree has developed unique characteristics to enhance their ability to survive and thrive. Therefore, when used as an essence, the shoot of a plant for instance, may elicit a creative awakening or potential unfolding.

The blueprint for forming these characteristics is found in each of the plant's components. An essence contains them as messages that rebalance emotions and/or attitudes. When a person has a negative or faulty message pattern, the appropriate essence can encourage correction. These messages have been found to be as beneficial to animals as to humans.

By their very nature, essences put us in touch with the natural environment and who we really are by creating harmony and balance. They can strengthen our overall energy and bring well-being emotionally, mentally, physically and spiritually.

Flower essences are a powerful and safe catalyst for change. They can help us live happier lives by transforming negative emotions and turning them into healthy patterns, affecting not only our health, but our relationships with others.

Because they are gentle in their action, essences do not conflict with conventional medicines or any other therapies.

Essence Remedies

Generally, essence remedies are taken for a month but they may be prescribed for up to three months. This will depend on the essence and the patient's response. Some people may be sensitive to a treatment, so the amount of remedy would need to be built up slowly so they can tolerate it and process it appropriately.

Sometimes, the dosage needs to be altered during treatment. This depends on the individual and the extent of the problem. Discuss what to expect from the individual essence with your natural therapist.

Change can occur in increments and it may take a few weeks to gauge subtle differences.

To make a diagnosis, a practitioner will ask a range of questions and listen carefully to both the answer and the way the person expresses themselves in order to ascertain the appropriate remedies. Often a client will gravitate towards a specific flower or plant, choosing intuitively.

How to Make Essences

There are many different types of essences and they are simply made by floating the plant parts in spring water in sunlight for a period of time. Once the essence has been created it is combined with a preservative such as ethanol. This is the mother essence, which is stored and from it smaller stock bottles are dispensed.

A complex of different essences may be prescribed to treat a particular condition but generally you would combine no more than five.

In herbal medicine, it is the plant or a part of the plant that is ingested by the patient whereas with flower essences, the solution contains the plant's energy but not any part of the actual plant.

How to Take Essences

Many essences are taken orally. Some are topically applied to the wrist. This method helps to acclimatise the person to the essence gently. This is especially important if a person has not used essences before or cannot tolerate alcohol, which is used as a preservative in some preparations.

Note: If the practitioner knows that the client has difficulty with alcohol, the essence can be prepared without it.

Essences can be bought already mixed into creams, or you can buy a fragrance free carrier cream and place a few drops of the essence into it yourself. Just mix it through and use it as an external treatment.

Some people find it helpful to focus on the positive qualities of the essence and visualise their symptoms lifting as they ingest the remedy. The majority of essences have an identified and applicable word and affirmation. These can be of great benefit because through repetition a whole new belief system can be created.

The remedies should be taken regularly and on rising and retiring is best because your mind is usually relaxed and receptive. Placing them next to the bed can help you remember to take it at those times.

It is important to take them 30 minutes before food or one hour after food.

Generally peppermint, chewing gum, lollies, mint toothpaste and coffee should be avoided when taking essences. Use non-peppermint toothpaste for the duration of taking the remedy.

Keep essences away from computers, mobile phones and magnetic devices, all of which emit electromagnetic radiation and can affect the vibration of the remedy. They should not sit in direct sunlight or be taken with food.

Getting to the Essence of Insomnia – Remedies

Following are some remedies from a series of essence ranges. Think about their qualities and investigate them further if you think they might be helpful for you.

Dr Ian White's Bush Flowers
Black eyed Susan
- Benefits people who are fast moving and think a lot. This kind of person becomes impatient with others who do not do things as fast as them. The person who will benefit from this remedy tries to cram too many activities into their waking hours. They need to contemplate and reduce the amount of stress in their lives

Crowea flower
- Especially pertinent for people to whom business, money and power is of enormous importance. The flower is linked with emotional balance and the stomach, where we digest nutrients and our experiences

Boronia

- Helps to turn off incessant dialogue in the mind; making it a clean slate to allow the person to sleep
- Promotes inner calm

Electro combination essence

- Releases the ill effects of electromagnetic radiation

For more information about Dr Ian White's Bush Flower essences go to: www.ausflowers.com.au

Bach Flower Essences

Impatients

- Aids people with a highly tense, stressed approach to life, leading to exhaustion

White chestnut

- Helps constant churning and over activity of the mind that often results in insomnia
- Helpful for those who sleep fitfully or experience general restlessness

Rescue remedy sleep

- The traditional Rescue Remedy is combined with White Chestnut Rescue Remedy, which assists with calming the mind and getting rid of unwanted thoughts. The formula contains 5 remedies that promote relaxation and assist with shock and trauma

Rock rose

- Helps people who suffer from nightmares or other experiences that bring a sense of deep emotional disturbance

Fes North American Essences

Chamomile
- Aids nervousness, hyperactivity and releases emotional tension held in the stomach
- Assists people to let go of the cares of the day
- Helps overcome insomnia

Lavender
- Aids a nervous disposition caused by over stimulation

Nasturtium
- For people who overwork and use their intellect too much causing brain fatigue or mental debility

Morning glory
- A good remedy for those who rely heavily on sedatives and stimulants, sleep poorly as a result and find it hard to wake in the morning
- It is also useful if the internal body clock is askew due to travel or shift work

St John's wort
- A helpful remedy for those who experience distress while sleeping in the form of night sweats, disturbing dreams and bed wetting

Yarrow environmental solution
- Provides a strong energetic shield to nourish and protect both our physical and non-physical immunity against electromagnetic fields

For more information about these essences go to: www.fesflowers.com

Falling Leaf Essences
Willow pattern tree
- ✦ This essence is helpful for anxiety based nervous insomnia caused by excessive mental activity
- ✦ Also for people who constantly turn things over in their mind or 'stew over' something. These people do not let their mind rest; they are busy thinking all the time
- ✦ Taking this essence on an hourly basis will lessen excessive mental activity that might otherwise prevent or detract from a good night's sleep
- ✦ Willow pattern tree essence promotes drowsiness and sleep

Sacred ulan
- ✦ Promotes sleep by lowering the heart rate and slowing down the breathing to appropriate levels
- ✦ In the mental realm it brings a calming effect to constant brain chatter, allowing the mind to relax

Pin oak
- ✦ Addresses fatigue caused by mental stress and exhaustion
- ✦ Slows excessive, irrelevant thought patterns and relaxes the mind
- ✦ Has a regenerative effect on the nervous system

Cockspur hawthorn
- ✦ Snorers and their partners will be grateful for cockspur hawthorn as it assists with temporary or chronic snoring

Scarlet oak bark
- ✦ Protects against electromagnetic radiation from computers and other every day technologies as well as electronic ley lines and other negative earth energies

To find out more about Falling leaf essences go to: www.advancedalchemy.com.au

Aromatherapy

What are essential oils?

The way to good health is to have an aromatic bath and scented massage every day.

– Hippocrates

A massage every day, ah what a treat! If only it were possible. However, for those of us who cannot partake in a daily rub down, you can still deploy some deliciously calming oils into your life to send you into a state of blissful calm.

Essential oils are highly concentrated volatile aromatic substances extracted from a plant part or its fruit, such as the rind of a lemon and orange. These oils are often referred to as the hormones or life force of the plant.

Aromatherapy is the art of using essential oils and their aromas as a form of therapy. The term aromatherapy was coined early last century by French chemist Dr R.H. Gattafosse who was involved in considerable scientific research into the properties of essential oils.

How Essential Oils Work?

The oils enter the body and take effect via two main routes, the nose and skin. Our sense of smell has a profound effect and influences us even though we may not be aware of it.

When we inhale them, tiny particles are taken to the roof of the nose where the olfactory system is located. Here, the thin hairs (cilia) transmit information to the olfactory bulb, situated behind the eyes. The olfactory bulb is the part of the brain that is involved in detecting odour. Smell signals are then decoded and sent on throughout the body to start a process of clearing toxicity and/or healing.

Essential oils can permeate the skin and enter the blood stream. They have a tiny molecular structure, minute enough to permeate the skin via the hair follicles and pores. From there the molecules are carried through the bloodstream via tiny blood carrying capillaries.

Ways to Apply Essential Oils

Massage

An effective way of receiving the benefits of essential oils is massage because the oils are absorbed into a larger area of the skin. At the same time the muscles are being relaxed, which helps to move the oil through the body.

Add to that the comforting effect of touch. Massage is a pleasurable experience to share with someone. However, this is not always convenient or possible. In this case you can massage yourself by rubbing the oils into those parts of your body that are reachable.

Inhalation

Place 2-4 drops of essential oil on a tissue or handkerchief and inhale several times when required.

Place 1 drop on a tissue and put that under your pillow case. Make sure it is not near your eyes.

Note: these methods should not be used for children.

Vapouriser

When essential oils are gently heated using a ceramic oil burner, they turn from liquid to vapour. These are the vapours you smell when you come close to a fragrant flower.

Vapours provide a therapeutic effect whilst you go about your daily routines. Often you may not be aware of the aroma at all, but it will still be doing its job.

Dilution

Fill the saucer of the burner with warm water and add 6-8 drops of your blend. Light the candle beneath.

Note that the water will evaporate after a few hours and will need to be refilled. Make sure that you place the burner in a safe place, away from children and curtains. Also do not leave a burner on while you are sleeping.

You can also purchase electric oil burners, which are very effective.

Aromatic baths and footbaths are other ways in which to absorb the benefits of essential oils.

Compress

Using a cold or warm compress soaked in essential oils is also a soothing regime for headaches and fever or on the abdomen for menstrual cramping.

Fold a clean hand towel, immerse the cloth in the water and then squeeze out the excess water and place on the required area such as your forehead.

Dilution

Fill a hand basin with water of the desired temperature and add 6-8 drops (2 drops for children) of the essential oil blend. Agitate the water vigorously to mix the oil.

How to Make Your Own Oil Mixture

It is easy to create your own mixture of essential oils. Because they are strong they need to be mixed with a carrier oil. Carrier or base oils play an important role in carrying or diluting the highly concentrated essential oils.

Carrier oils play a number of roles. They inhibit the evaporation rate of the essential oils, make them easier to spread evenly over the skin and encourage quick absorption.

Cold pressed oils are an ideal medium for massage as well as cosmetics as they are rich in nutrients. They are also ideal for most dry and sensitive skin types.

Following is a list of some of the beneficial cold pressed oils to use with essential oils:

- *Sweet almond is* the best off all purpose carrier because it is neutral, non-allergenic and less expensive than the others. It is lovely to use for massaging babies
- *Avocado* oil is drawn from the flesh of the avocado and is high in vitamins A, C and E
- *Olive oil* is a lighter emollient oil that is easily absorbed into the skin
- *Sesame oil* warmed up is easily absorbed into the skin and has a detoxifying action that draws out impurities. It is very soothing and a good moisturiser

Dilutions for adults:

- 50 ml or 10 teaspoons carrier oil to 25 drops of essential oil, or
- 10 ml or 2 teaspoons of carrier oil to 5 drops of essential oil

Dilutions for children:

- 15 ml carrier oil to 2 drops essential oil

Insomnia Relief

Lavander (Lavandula angustifolia)

Lavender is a well known relaxant. It is harmonising and balancing to the body. It helps to relieve irritability, nervous tension, mild anxiety and stress and is useful for calming irritable children. It can also assist in the relief of cold and flu symptoms, insomnia and headaches.

Effects:

- Relaxing
- Refreshing
- Balancing
- Soothing
- Calming
- Antifungal
- Antibacterial

Place 5 drops of lavender oil in water in an oil burner to infuse the room with the aroma. Before bed, make sure the tea light is extinguished.

Lemon (Citrus lemon)

Lemon assists the relief of nervous tension, stress and mild anxiety and it can be helpful in relieving insomnia. Because it has calming properties it can refresh the mind and help with exhaustion, mental fatigue and nervous tension. Inhaling lemon oil can help concentration.

Effects:

- Uplifting
- Cooling
- Refreshing

- ✦ Enlivening
- ✦ Antiseptic
- ✦ Astringent for skin toning
- ✦ Insect repellent

Orange (sweet) (Citrus aurantium)

Insomnia that is brought on by stress can be assisted with orange oil. It can also relieve anger, anxiety and depression.

Effects:

- ✦ Soothing and gentle
- ✦ Uplifting and refreshing
- ✦ Relieves nervous tension so it is beneficial in times of stress and mild anxiety
- ✦ Gentle treatment for irritability in children
- ✦ Temporary relief from sleeplessness
- ✦ Treating/relieving cold, flu and bronchial cough symptoms
- ✦ Antiseptic

Sandalwood (Santalum album)

Sandalwood is an ancient oil used for more than 4,000 years for religious and healing purposes. It can reduce inflammation, anxiety, fear, stress and restlessness and enhance relaxation and concentration.

Effects:

- ✦ Relaxing
- ✦ Sedating
- ✦ Calming
- ✦ Strengthening
- ✦ Relief of nervous tension, stress and mild anxiety

- Temporary relief of sleeplessness
- Temporary relief of sore throat and laryngitis
- Anti-spasmodic
- Antiseptic

Ylang Ylang (Canangaodorata)

Ylang Ylang is a body balancing essence that is useful in relieving stress, nervous tension and mild anxiety as well as being a relaxant so it can assist with the symptoms of insomnia.

Effects:

- Sedating
- Relaxing
- Warming
- Pacifying
- Enlivening
- Euphoria
- Antiseptic

This essential oil should be used sparingly. If it is used in high doses it can cause nausea, headaches and drowsiness.

Clary sage (Salvia sclarea)

Clary sage helps relieve symptoms of premenstrual tension and stress.

Effects:

- Calming
- Relaxing
- Warming
- Antiseptic

Place 6 drops of clary sage in an oil burner to infuse the room with the essential oil.

Before bed make sure that the tea light is extinguished.

Frankincense (Olibanum boswellia)

Frankincense helps relieve nervous tension and stress.

Effects:

- ✦ Calming
- ✦ Soothing
- ✦ Relaxing
- ✦ Anti-inflammatory to the skin

Place 6 drops of frankincense in an oil burner to infuse the room with the essential oil.

Make sure that the tea light is extinguished before bed.

Geranium rose (Pelagonium graveolens)

Geranium rose helps in the relief of nervous tension and mild anxiety.

Effects:

- ✦ Balancing
- ✦ Calming
- ✦ Astringent
- ✦ Antiseptic
- ✦ Uplifting

This is such an uplifting oil that it is good to carry it around with you for whenever you need a boost. Place 25 drops of rose geranium in 50ml of carrier oil and place in a clean glass bottle.

Massage on skin externally.

Marjoram (Origanum marjorana)

Marjoram oil can calm the emotions and relieve stress, anxiety and hyperactivity.

Effects:

+ Warming
+ Relaxing
+ Assists in the relief of cramping
+ Assists in the relief of muscular aches

Place 2-4 drops of marjoram oil in 20ml of carrier cream and massage onto the legs before bed.

Caution

Avoid use during early pregnancy.

Some Super Relaxing Essential Oil Combinations

These combinations can be massaged into your arms, legs and torso, and wherever else you can reach, before bed.

Essential combo 1

+ 3 drops of lavender
+ 2 drops of sandalwood
+ 2 drops of geranium
+ 20 ml of carrier oil

Essential combo 2

+ 3 drops of lavender
+ 3 drops of orange
+ 3 drops of marjoram
+ 20 ml of carrier oil

Essential combo 3
- 1 drop Ylang Ylang
- 4 drops orange
- 2 drops geranium

or
- 4 drops orange
- 3 drops of lavender
- 2 drops of geranium

To de-stress and relieve nervous tension

Combine:
- 2 drops frankincense
- 2 drops clary sage
- 2 drops geranium
- 20 ml of carrier oil

Homoeopathy

The word homoeopathy is derived from two Greek words, 'homoeo', meaning 'like' and 'pathos', meaning 'suffering'. The principle of homoeopathy is based on the law of similars, that is, what a substance can cause it can also cure if given in sufficiently small amounts.

German physician, Dr Samuel Hahnemann, developed homoeopathy around 200 years ago. He tested medicines on healthy people and found that each substance produced specific symptoms.

When the same substances were administered in tiny doses to a sick person who was displaying similar symptoms, the illness would be cured by stimulating the body's own healing process. For example, if a person was suffering from a headache, giving a small amount of the substance that was able to cause the headache would also be able to dispel it.

Thousands of substances have now been prepared for use as homoeopathic medicines and it is safe to administer to all ages from babies to the elderly.

Hahnemann found that the more a remedy was diluted the greater its potency. In some homoeopathic remedies, only the vibration of the original substance remains. Because of the extent of the dilution, toxicity and drug interactivity problems are avoided.

In homoeopathy, the whole person is treated, not the illness. The idea is that if you make the person well, the illness has nowhere to dwell. In a consultation, very detailed case histories are taken including past and present mental and emotional experiences as well as physical symptoms.

No thought, feeling or symptom is too insignificant for the homoeopath to note in order to gain an understanding of the patterns of the individual's psychology and physiology. On this basis, a single homoeopathic remedy is prescribed. In subsequent consultations responses to the medicine will be assessed and the individual's case will be further explored.

Types of Homoeopathy

A number of different styles of homoeopathy are practiced throughout the world. *Classical homoeopathy*, the form created by Samuel Hahnemann, involves painstaking attention to the details of the client's presentation and the prescription of a single homoeopathic remedy to match that picture.

Another style is called *poly-pharmacy* or mixing various remedies together to form a compound remedy.

Constitutional homoeopathy takes reference from the persons inherited predispositions, past illnesses, diet, general reactions to the environment, intellectual and emotional features, general attitude to life as well as body shape, character and personality. Only one remedy is offered in constitutional homoeopathy.

Another type of treatment used is where *miasms* (a fundamental underlying problem or illness that does not resolve or shift), are recognised and hereditary conditions are taken into account.

Homoeopathic Treatments for Insomnia

For the best result, a therapist should prescribe homoeopathics although there are some over the counter insomnia remedies that generally have a mixture of avena, passiflora and valeriana for relaxing the mind. These formulas are safe to use but you will always get the best results from a tailor made mixture.

Following are a list of homoeopathic remedies and the conditions they affect. These are all short term remedies and should be prescribed by an experienced homoeopath.

If there is no improvement within three weeks, consult again with your homoeopath who will revise your treatment.

Common oat (Avena sativa)

Avena sativa is made from the common oat and has a sedative action on the brain and nervous system.

Assists with:

- ✦ Nervous exhaustion and sleeplessness
- ✦ Performance anxiety
- ✦ A mind that cannot focus on any one subject

Passion flower (Passiflora incarnata)

The dried passion flower has a history of use in cases of insomnia as a sedative and hypnotic. It is also helpful for gastrointestinal complaints related to nervousness. Passiflora has a calming action.

Assists with:

- Quieting the nervous system
- Restless sleep and wakefulness due to exhaustion
- Overwork, worries and self doubt

Valeriana (Valerian)

Valerian is generally known as a herb that helps induce sleep.

Assists with:

- Sleeplessness with night itching and muscular spasms, which are worse on waking
- Extremities that are affected by rheumatic pains in limbs as well as constant jerking
- Oversensitivity and irritability

Phosphate of magnesia (Magnesia phosphorica)

Magnesia is an excellent anti spasmodic remedy.

Assists with:

- Cramping muscles with radiating pain
- Neuralgic pains which are relieved by warmth
- Tiredness, lethargy and exhaustion
- Sleeplessness due to indigestion
- Cramps in calves, general muscular weakness

Yellow lady's slipper orchid (Cypripedium pubescens)

This elegant plant with a slipper like flower was traditionally used by the North American Indians for nervous tension. It is a useful sedative and relaxant.

Assists with:

- Nervous and irritated conditions, especially in women with restlessness and twitching of the body
- Children who laugh and play in the night

Ignatia (Ignatia amara)

This is a profound remedy for grief and anguish. It is useful for people who are under a lot of stress. The healing properties are derived from a small bean that grows inside the fruit of the plant.

Assists with:

- Feelings of defensiveness
- Excessive yawning and inability to sleep
- Dreading not being able to sleep
- When sleep comes so do nightmares
- Feelings that are easily hurt and offended
- Back spasms, cramps, drawing pains, related to the experience of emotional stress
- Insomnia and regular sleepiness
- Clinical depression
- Chronic fatigue syndrome
- Headache
- Muscular spasms

Hyoscyamus (Hyoscyamus niger)

This herb is otherwise known as henbane. This remedy is specifically for the nervous system.

Assists with:

- Being argumentative
- Hyperactivity
- Feeling of light headedness and confusion
- A feeling of vertigo as if intoxicated
- Vascular cramps, spasms and convulsions
- Extreme restlessness
- Being unable to sleep
- Muscle twitches over the whole body
- Cramps in calves and toes
- Intense sleepiness

Coffea (Coffea arabic)

This homoeopathic remedy is made from the coffee bean and is useful for depression and sleeplessness.

Assists with:

- Heightened activity of the mind as well as restlessness, sensitivity and nervous agitation
- Uncontrollable thoughts and a racing mind
- Sleeping until 3am, then just dozing for the rest of the night
- Being sleepless due to mental activity
- Waking up with a start
- Sleep that is disturbed by dreams
- Being constantly on the move

Cocculus (Cocculus indicus)

This remedy is used mainly for the central nervous system, where there is a fundamental weakness.

Assists with:

- Low energy resulting from lack of sleep or sadness
- Effects of grief and anger
- Motion sickness
- Hysteria
- Over stimulation of the nervous system
- Especially useful for insomnia during menopause

Nat mur (Natrium muriaticum)

This remedy, made from sodium chloride or rock salt, helps remove grief.

Assists with:

- Blame
- Grief
- Lack of sleep due to being upset
- When a person cannot fall asleep because of their grief or unpleasant feelings from the distant past
- Nervous jerking during sleep

Poison nut (Nux vomica)

This remedy is made from the seeds of the strychnos tree, which is the source of strychnine.

Assists with:

- Sleeplessness caused by mental strain
- Inability to sleep because of overindulging in rich food

- Withdrawal from alcohol or sleeping tablets
- Hangovers (overindulgence in alcohol)
- Waking between 3am and 4am and falling asleep just as it is time to get up
- Nightmares
- Daytime irritability

Pulsatilla (Pulsatilla nigricans)

This remedy is made from the windflower and is suitable for many female related disorders.

Assists with:

- Restlessness in women during the first stage of sleep
- Women who feel too hot in bed and throw the covers off, then start to feel too cold
- Insomnia due to persistent thoughts
- Feeling wide awake in the evenings

Chamomilla (Matricaria chamomilla)

Chamomilla is useful for intolerance to pain. It is sometimes known as a baby sitter in a bottle as it helps to settle whiny children.

Assists with:

- Children who are feeling wide awake and irritable, during the first part of the night
- Children who want to be carried around all the time

Arsenicum (Arsenicum album)

This remedy is derived from arsenic and is useful for a whole range of disorders including allergies, anxiety, depression and insomnia.

Assists with:

- Waking up between midnight and 2 am
- Restlessness
- Worry and apprehension
- Foreboding dreams of fire and danger

Rhus tox (Rhus toxicodendron)

We commonly know this remedy as 'poison ivy' and it is useful for a myriad of conditions such as rheumatism, aches caused by flu, as well as restlessness and sleeplessness caused by pain that is experienced when lying down.

Assists with:

- Being unable to sleep
- Irritability and restless
- Having to walk about during the night because of pain and discomfort

Aurum (Aurum metallicum)

This is helpful for those who suffer deep depression and lack a feeling of connection to life.

Assists with:

- Dreams about dying
- Night time hunger
- Problems at work
- Good for those who are depressed because of work related issues

Soaking in Healing Waters

There is nothing like settling into a hot steamy bath for unwinding after a long day, to soak out the toxins and stress and to relax the mind and body. The bath provides a luxurious haven plus a therapeutic medium.

Bathing is an ancient tradition. Water, the symbol of cleansing, purification and enchantment, has been celebrated by the ancient Hindus, Sumerians, Indians and North American Navajo cultures.

Water was considered to be a great healer, a symbol of nature, and has been a theme of myths and stories for centuries.

It therefore seems perfectly natural to seek refuge, peace and equilibrium in water. We submerge and release our bodies and minds to watery comfort. Today, in many western homes a spa bath is installed in bathrooms as a symbol of luxury.

Create your own spa retreat in your bathroom prior to bedtime. Light the bathroom with aromatherapy scented candles. Drop aromatherapy oils such as lavender in the bath and you have an ambient space in which to 'holiday' for the next 20 minutes.

Cleopatra Bath

Bath therapy consists of a course of seven baths taken twice a week for three and a half weeks. It is ideal for children and adults who have food allergies, lack appetite, are tired and stressed from working too hard, or from exams, and women whose energy is depleted from breast feeding.

Make it a lovely ritual; something to look forward to.

Preparations

- Make sure that the bathroom is free of drafts
- Spread a towel or woollen blanket on the bed
- Run a bath that is 37 degrees celsius (you can use a normal thermometer to gauge the temperature)
- In a container combine well 500ml of non-homogenised milk*, 1 egg and a dessert spoon of honey
- Pour into the bath

The child can enjoy being immersed in the water with only their head exposed for 10-12 minutes in winter and 15 minutes in summer.

After the bath

- Help the child out of the bath
- Do not dry them, just drape a towel around their shoulders and have another towel to wrap around their head
- Carry the child to the bed and wrap them in the towel or blanket on the bed so that they are totally enveloped and no skin is in contact with the bed. Only the face is exposed
- Cover them with a doona or blankets
- Sit with them and read or tell a story that is uplifting and beautiful or meditative
- They can lay there for 20 minutes or if they fall asleep let them be for as long as possible. If it is night time they can be left to sleep through the night. If the towels are wet then put the child in their pyjamas.
- If the bath is taken during the day then they should resume normal activities after the 20 minute bed rest

---

*You can get non-homogenised milk from health food shops and some supermarkets.

For adults, when you come out of the bath, pat yourself dry and play relaxing music while lying covered on your bed.

Sometimes a child or adult may cry or feel anger when they have one of these baths. It does not happen very often but it is not a bad thing. The baths can help an emotional issue to rise to the surface and this is positive as it is releasing bad feelings. After 2-3 baths this will resolve itself.

Aromatic bath

Having an aromatherapy bath is a triple treat. It is luxuriously relaxing, and you inhale the oils as well as absorb them through your skin.

Method

Close the doors and windows, place a small towel that has been dipped into the bathwater and wrung out, under your neck to support it rather than having to strain your neck while lying back on the hard porcelain. Breathe deeply and enjoy for 10-20 minutes.

Dilution

Use 6-8 drops of a blend of essential oils to suit (use 2 drops for children). Add the oils to the bath water immediately before immersing. Agitate the water vigorously to disperse the oil.

Tip: If you do not have time for a bath you can still bathe in essential oils by applying them in a carrier oil and massaging them into your body before a shower. Alternatively, placing a few drops of the oil on the shower floor will allow the essence to be infused by the steam of the shower.

Warm Brew

A warm bath before retiring is a tonic. Not only does it feels good, it also helps to increase circulation to the skin and it relaxes the muscles. Following are some bath recipes to send you into a state of blissful peace.

Bath Infusions

Bath recipe 1
Combine one heaped teaspoon of dried lavender and one heaped teaspoon of rosemary. Both herbs have relaxing properties. These herbs can be scooped into a thin cotton bag or clean stocking that is tied off at the end and placed into the warm bath to steep like a tea bag.

Squeeze your herbal bouquet to release more of the properties into the bath water.

Submerge yourself in the warm water.

Do not let the bath get cold, either add more hot water or get out.

Bath recipe 2
Use 5 drops of basil oil or make an infusion by placing dried basil inside a cloth bag or sock and steep it in the bath. Basil is good for releasing muscle tension and enhancing mental clarity.

Bath recipe 3
Place 5 drops of lavender oil or an infusion of dried lavender in a cloth bag and steep it in the bath.

Bath recipe 4
If you have muscular aches and pains, place a handful of Epsom salts or baking soda into the bath. This will help to relax the muscles and soothe nerves on the surface of the skin.

Best Foot Forward

Many nerve endings are found in the soles of the feet. A foot bath is a great way to relax the whole body because of the interconnection between the nerve endings through the spinal cord and up to the brain. So once the feet are relaxed, the brain relaxes. Therefore, having warm feet also helps restore mental clarity because it relaxes the head.

The head and feet are areas where much body heat is lost, so maintaining stable heat helps the body function well.

The benefits of a footbath are enormous; especially when there is no full bath available. Oils are absorbed very effectively through the feet and it is a pampering experience. They can relieve cramps in the feet and legs and assist with insomnia.

Use five drops of the oil of your choice in a footbath. Some suggestions:

- Lavender-for relaxation
- Rosemary-helps soothe restless feet and promotes immunity

Foot bath 1

Use a bathtub or some other large container, such as a large bucket.

Fill the vessel with warm water and increase the temperature until it is as hot as you can tolerate (around 41 degrees Celsius).

Soak the feet for 20 minutes.

When the water cools down, add some more boiling water to maintain the temperature.

Dry the feet with a towel and keep them wrapped up and warm for about 15 minutes. It is beautifully relaxing and makes your feet feel lovely and soft.

Foot bath 2

Another method is to fill a bowl with warm water and place a layer of marbles across the bottom. Add 4-6 drops of an essential oil blend (2 drops for children) and agitate the water to mix the oils.

As you relax and soak your feet, gently roll them across the marbles. There is extra benefit as the marbles stimulate the nerve endings on the soles of the feet.

Foot bath 3

Have a footbath with sea salt or an organic lemon cut and squeezed under the water or nettle. This can clear heavy headedness and relax the body. It is also good for immunity and for helping to clear the stuffiness of head colds.

The quieter you become the more you can hear.

– Baba Ram Dass

Thought Field Therapy

Thought Field Therapy (TFT) is an emotional healing therapy that is based on the principle that when a person experiences any kind of thought, be it good or negative and limiting, such as fears or upsets, a thought field is created.

Around 23 years ago, Roger Callahan PhD, a leading American clinical research psychologist developed TFT. He took the principal of meridians or energy pathways known through acupuncture, and developed a systematic set of techniques for the treatment of emotional problems. To this, he employed principals of modern science, acupressure, kinesiology and the body's energy system.

Dr Callahan understood that problems resulted from disturbances or upsets in the thought field. These are what he referred to as 'perturbations' or disturbances in our energy systems or meridians.

How TFT Works

When we think about a negative experience, problem or fear, the thought field contains specific patterns that become active while we think about the problem. This creates the emotional distress referred to as a 'perturbation', being something that perturbs.

Each perturbation corresponds to a specific acupressure point on the body. To eliminate the upset, a precise sequence of acupressure points is physically tapped with the fingers.

Different tapping sequences called 'algorithms' are used to address different issues with the aim of unblocking and rebalancing the flow of qi or life energy. This serves to free you from the negative emotion.

Patients notice a rapid and dramatic improvement in the way they feel and the results are long lasting.

TFT is a natural, drug free and non-invasive therapy that is effective for eliminating the following emotions, which in themselves can contribute to insomnia:

- Fear
- Anxiety
- Phobias
- Stress
- Guilt
- Rage and anger
- Depression
- Trauma
- Grief
- Obsession
- Physical addictions and withdrawal symptoms

Removing Insomnia from the Thought Field

TFT can assist with anxiety, which can lead to insomnia. There is a particular exercise called 'collarbone breathing' to relieve this, which should be used on waking in the morning and before retiring for sleep at night.

When the therapist guides you through this series of tapping exercises on different points on the face, hands and body, a sense of release is evident through signs such as sighing and yawning. The tapping causes a feeling of relaxation.

For more information view Dr Callahan's website: www.rogercallahan.com

Collarbone Breathing Exercise

Collarbone breathing can balance the bioenergy system (that is our electrical, qi and autonomic central nervous system) and resolve some of the emotional stressors that contribute to insomnia at a deep level.

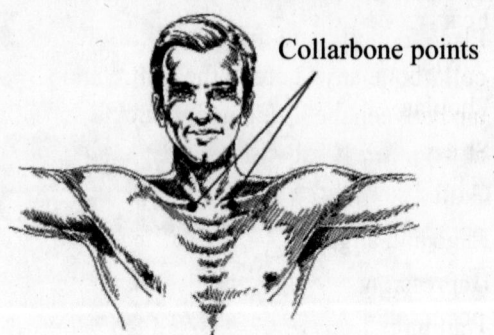

Fig. 16.1 *Collarbone Points*

Collarbone breathing is very effective for insomnia, however, the 'common anxiety sequence' is often very helpful for reducing stress and recurring bad thoughts. It also causes a person to relax, hence its usefulness in assisting the act of going to sleep or going back to sleep.

✦ The collarbone points are located 2-4 inches at either side of the base of the throat under the collarbone

Breathing Positions

+ There are 5 breathing positions in this exercise:
    (1) Breathe normally
    (2) Take a deep breath in fully and hold it
    (3) Let half that breath out and hold it
    (4) Let it all out and hold it
    (5) Take half a breath in and hold it and then breath out

Touching Positions

For the whole of this exercise you will be tapping between your little finger knuckle and ring finger knuckle. It is important not to take your hands off that area throughout the entire sequence.

+ Place the left hand index and middle finger under the right collarbone anywhere in the centre and with your right hand tap between the little finger knuckle and ring finger knuckle of your left hand with your right index and middle finger. At the same time go through the 5 breathing positions (as per above)
+ Tap rapidly about 5 good taps for each of the breathing positions.
+ Then, slide the same 2 fingertips of the left hand to the left collarbone and repeat the above 5 breathing positions whilst tapping rapidly with your right hand fingers for about 5 good taps for each of the breathing positions
+ Now, make a fist out of the left hand, which is still sitting under the left collarbone, continue tapping between the little finger and ring finger knuckle and start the breathing positions again

- Then, slide the left hand fist to the right under the collarbone, continue tapping with your right hand and start the breathing positions
- Now place the right hand index and middle finger under your right collarbone and tap between the little finger knuckle and ring finger knuckle with your left hand index and middle finger. At the same time go through the 5 breathing positions
- Then slide the same 2 fingertips of the right hand to the underside of your left collarbone. Continue tapping as you repeat the breathing positions
- Make a fist out of the right hand, which is still sitting under the left collarbone. Continue tapping and repeat the 5 breathing positions
- Slide your right fist across to the underside of the right collarbone. Continue the tapping and repeat the breathing positions

Behavioural Therapy

Cognitive behavioural therapy (CBT) is a psychological therapy used by many clinical psychologists, psychiatrists and counselors to help change thoughts, feelings and behaviours such as anxiety, depression, relationship problems, eating disorders and insomnia.

The approach is based on the idea that how you think (cognition) and act (behaviour) affects the way you feel.

Generally, CBT is used to assist in the treatment of psychological conditions, including depression, panic attacks, anxiety, eating disorders and substance abuse. When it comes to insomnia, it can help change the thoughts and actions that interfere with the ability to achieve restful sleep.

Studies have shown that psychological and behavioural factors play an important role in insomnia and that CBT can be effective in treating them and improving sleep sustainably.

How CBT Works

The 'cognitive' aspect of the therapy teaches you to recognise and change false beliefs that affect your ability to sleep and the 'behavioural' element helps you develop good sleep hygiene tools to assist you reach specific goals and indeed gain more control over your life. This approach can work well if a person is entrenched in a chronic non-sleeping pattern.

A behavioural therapist will help you determine your sleep goals and then look at the specific actions needed to remove the obstacles to achieving a good night's sleep, such as:

- Using the bedroom for sleep and not studying or watching television
- Changing your body's response to stress, that is, not lying awake worrying about stuff
- Incorrect perceptions about sleep, for example, some people believe that they must have eight hours or they cannot function, whereas, as you get older you may only need seven
- Where illness is a cause of insomnia, one must learn to manage and cope with the illness

Behavioural therapy for sleep starts with good sleep hygiene, which includes daytime behaviour. Preparing your mind and body by staying mentally and physically healthy is a helpful first step for any endeavour, sleep included.

Behavioural Therapy Techniques

Following are some examples of some of the behavioural therapy techniques that may alleviate insomnia:

Ways of gaining control

Association

+ A person with insomnia who associates the bed and bedroom with a whole range of activities, such as watching television and studying, needs to learn to re-associate it with rapid sleep onset. This method is effective in situations where the bed and bedroom is associated with poor sleep.

Muscle relaxation techniques

+ For people who are highly stimulated day and night, progressive muscle relaxation techniques are really useful. Travelling from the feet up, different muscle groups are progressively tensed and relaxed. If you are feeling tense during the day you can take a few minutes sitting in your chair at the desk to do this one.

Facing the fear

+ A method known as 'paradoxical intention' involves persuading a patient to actually engage in their most feared behaviour such as lying awake. They are given strategies to deal with the anxiety and in turn eliminate it.

Reading the signs

+ Biofeedback operates on the idea that we can influence certain automatic body functions by using our minds. A patient is hooked up to a machine that measures physical reactions to stress through sensors that record muscle contractions and skin temperature. Many sleep disturbances are related to stress, which in turn sparks up the fight or flight response. Biofeedback can teach a person to control involuntary processes through recognising the stress responses such as increased heart rate; therefore, they can learn to control the stress symptoms.

Beyond belief

✦ Cognitive therapy helps correct faulty beliefs and attitudes about sleep. A strategy suited to the individual will be developed or drawn from a number of techniques.

Buteyko

The Buteyko method of breathing is most renowned for assisting people with asthma. However, it is very effective in reducing snoring, sleep apnoea and other breathing disorders. Buteyko is a method of training people to breathe more effectively.

The method was discovered by Russian doctor Konstantin Pavlovich Buteyko in the late 1940's. At the time, he was a medical student with an assignment to observe patients' breathing rates in relation to the severity and prognosis of their illness. He discovered a link between dying and depth of breath; that depth of breathing increased as a person was dying.

He concluded that there was an association between these two factors; that a patient's condition deteriorated as their breathing depth increased. Conversely, those who reduced or normalised their breathing began to recover. Dr Buteyko reasoned that if there really was a connection between hyperventilation and illness it should be possible to reverse this with deliberate breath control.

His study of yoga texts enlightened him about breath restriction exercises. He experimented on himself and with patients. Thus, the Buteyko method was born. His research into dysfunctional breathing and hyperventilation and its effects on the human body, as well as developing the breathing techniques, continued for more than 30 years.

Buteyko linked hyperventilation to several conditions, including asthma, sleep apnoea and snoring, and set about developing techniques to normalise breathing patterns, reversing symptoms and lessening the need for medication. His research describes why people hyperventilate, why it self-perpetuates and how to reverse the cycle.

His discovery has significantly changed the management and lifestyle of thousands of people with asthma, sleep apnoea, snoring and other breathing disorders.

Buteyko breathing workshops re-educate people about how to breathe. Exercises are given that take an hour each day and the results are recorded along with changes in sleeping, eating, medication intake and physical condition.

The Buteyko breathing retraining program provides immediate and significant improvement for people with asthma, sleep apnoea and other breathing-related conditions. It can improve quality of sleep, clear sinus problems, shorten the time you need to sleep and improve general health, stamina, endurance and sports performance. It also normalises both daytime and night-time breathing.

Over 90 per cent of people suffering from asthma who learn the method significantly reduce their need for asthma reliever medications within one week and if you live with a snorer you will notice a big difference in a very short time frame.

Buteyko course clients are advised that they should only alter prescribed medication in consultation with their medical practitioner.

Research

Double blind, randomised, controlled clinical asthma trials have shown excellent outcomes. Results of one asthma trial conducted by Buteyko Australia in conjunction with the Australian Associated Asthma Foundations showed:

- A 96 per cent reduction in the need for reliever medications for people who learned Buteyko
- A 49 per cent reduction in preventer medications
- Improvements in quality of life and less asthma symptoms

The control group who were not taught the Buteyko method showed no improvements.

Benefits/Outcomes

The Buteyko Institute method can enhance health in the following ways, depending on the current health status of the individual. Breathing re-training can:

- Significantly reduce asthma symptoms and the need for medication
- Improved tolerance of asthma triggers
- Reduce allergic reactions
- Improve quality of life because of enhanced health benefits
- Increase energy and stamina and enhanced sporting performance
- Improve the quality of sleep and reduce or eliminate snoring
- Improve ability to cope with stress
- Enhance the immune system so people are more resistant to illnesses

- Provides more energy and ability to exercise
- Reduce the need for a CPAP machine for people with sleep apnoea (this should be supervised by a doctor)
- Improved skin conditions such as dry skin or eczema
- Normalise weight that is, people who are overweight tend to lose some weight, while those who are underweight may gain some
- Reduce or eliminate headaches and migraines
- Reduce anxiety and panic attacks
- Improve thinking and concentration levels
- Reduce irritability and depression

How to Learn Buteyko Breathing

Buteyko is a safe, non-invasive technique that should be taught by a qualified practitioner. The Buteyko Institute follows international best practice medication guidelines.

For more information and to find a Buteyko practitioner, contact the Buteyko Institute of Breathing and Health at: www.buteyko.info.

Meditation

Meditation and Relaxation

> *Remember, if you can cease all restless activity, your integral nature will appear.*
>
> – Lao Tzu

What is Meditation?

Meditation is an ancient discipline described as the experience of the limitless nature of the mind. It is a practice that exists in almost every religious and cultural system in the world. We are very lucky to live in this time because the modern world offers many styles of meditation.

The benefits of meditation are manifold; it clears the constant mind chatter, calms and stills the mind, and keeps our attention anchored in the present. For some it is a doorway to connect with their higher consciousness and/or 'the source'.

In some forms of meditation the focus is on the breath to still our thoughts. By doing this we are not concerned with the past or worrying about the future. We are in the present, only breathing and 'being in the now'.

While in this state of heightened awareness we can respond with clarity and authority to everything in our lives. If we did one thing at a time in a focused and conscious manner throughout the day, while being cognisant of this awareness, our health (body, mind and spirit) would improve dramatically.

You can liken the experience of meditation to cleaning a window that's view has been obstructed due to the accumulation of years of dust. Once you begin to clean it you start to realise how limited your vision has been. You gaze through the immaculate glass and finally see the brilliance of the colours of the landscape, the sharpness of the roads and houses, and how interesting the passers-by are.

On the Right Wave Length

Unless you have been overindulging in alcohol, your brain will consist of billions of brain cells called neurons. Neurons communicate with each other via electricity. You can tell a lot about a person simply by observing their brainwave patterns. For example, anxious people tend to produce an overabundance of high Beta waves while people with depression tend to produce an overabundance of slower Alpha and Theta brainwaves.

Researchers have found that not only do brainwaves indicate mental state, they can be stimulated to change a person's mental state, and even help treat a variety of mental disorders.

Brainwaves have peaks, like the tips of waves. These are measured according to how many times they peak in one second (cycles per second). Electricity in India has 50 cycles per second.

There are 5 kinds of brainwaves identified and each of these has a pattern:

1. Beta waves are your conscious mind in action. These waves are active when you are awake, thinking, talking and problem solving (13-25 cycles per second).
2. Alpha waves are active when we are engaged in activities such as relaxing and meditating. This is a time when we are able to receive inspirational thoughts (8-12 cycles per second).
3. Theta waves are active during deep mediation. This brain wave is dominant in children from 2-5 years old. It is associated with imagination (4-8 cycles per second).
4. Delta waves occur when you are in a deep relaxed sleep. This is a time when you do not even dream (0.5-4 cycles per second).
5. Gamma waves have been identified more recently as having the most rapid frequency (20-80 cycles per second). Gamma waves are active during precognition, when a person processes high level information, when waking up, in the REM sleep stage and during meditation.

During the state of meditation, it is the only time when the left and right brain waves synchronise by peaking at the same time and scientists believe that this state provides us with greater mind power for creativity and learning.

Om! God I Feel Great

Science is now starting to catch up with what eastern cultures have understood and been practicing for thousands of years.

A number of studies have been conducted in recent years on the effect of meditation on the brain. Advances in brain imaging have made it possible to see which parts of the brain are stimulated and active when people are pondering, meditating or responding.

Neuroscientists have found that meditation shifts brain activity to different areas of the cortex. Brain waves that are focused in the stress prone right frontal cortex move to the calmer left frontal cortex.

This shift decreases the negative effects of stress, as well as mild depression and anxiety.

Monkeying Around with the Brain

One recent study that took place at the request of the Dalai Lama actually demonstrated that mental discipline and meditative practice can achieve different levels of awareness through changing the workings of the brain.

The Dalai Lama invited neuroscientist Dr Richard Davidson, from the W.M. Keck Laboratory for Functional Brain Imaging and Behaviour at the University of Wisconsin, to study the workings of the brains of eight of his most accomplished meditation practitioners.

The monks had between 10,000-50,000 meditation hours notched up under their saffron robes. This was compared to a control group of 10 volunteer students with no previous meditation experience.

Researchers at the University of Wisconsin hooked up the brains of the Tibetan monks, plus a control group, to magnetic imaging machines. Their cerebral experiences were translated into high frequency gamma waves.

After being fitted with 256 electrical sensors and meditating for short periods, both groups were then asked to meditate specifically on unconditional compassion. This goes to the heart of the Dalai Lama's teaching, that is, the 'unrestricted readiness and availability to help living beings.'

The results unambiguously showed that meditation activated the trained minds of the monks in significantly different ways from those of the volunteers. The electrodes picked up much greater activation of fast moving and unusually powerful gamma waves in the monks, and found that the movement of the waves through the brain was far better organised and coordinated than in the students.

The meditation novices showed only a slight increase in gamma wave activity while meditating. The monks who had spent the most years meditating had the highest levels of gamma waves and some of them produced gamma wave activity more powerful than any previously reported in a healthy person.

Gamma wave activity is associated with consciousness, perception and other mental activities such as focus, memory, learning and higher states of consciousness.

Other conclusions show that meditation not only changes the workings of the brain in the short term, but also quite possibly produces permanent changes. They also discovered that the brains of long term meditation practitioners are trained in a way that is likened to the way practicing a sport will improve performance. This demonstrates that the brain can be trained and modified.

This is a new way of thinking for brain scientists because there has been a long held belief that the brain's nerve cells could not be rewired, that they were fixed during childhood and never changed. This new concept of ongoing brain development is called 'neuroplasticity.'

Up, close and personal with Transcendental Meditation (TM)

More than 600 controlled studies have been carried out on the health benefits of TM. We know that it has the potential to improve the immune system, reduce stress and normalise blood pressure. Studies have shown that it even reverses the build up of plaque in coronary arteries.

What happens during TM is that there is a decrease in beta waves where information processing slows and an increase in theta waves (these are also activated when a person falls asleep). As the person becomes immersed in the waters of relaxation it diminishes negative feelings and increases levels of contentment.

It is a very powerful form of meditation and the effects impact your whole life.

Clearing the Path

A calm and clear mind is not focusing on current or past troubles or challenges. By taking this time to meditate you are at the least practicing stress reduction, which impacts your health and allows you to access your true, essential self aside from the roles you play in your daily life.

The process of meditation is also a deeply soothing experience no matter which type you learn. The idea is to focus your attention on a particular object of stimulus such as a mantra or the breath and exclude all other thoughts.

Meditation is a way of training the mind to create greater calm, which can bring increased insight into life experiences.

Once your mind begins to release itself from its constant chatter and noise it will respond with vitality and power as if peering through a newly polished window. You will find a whole new world open to you.

Do not Cogitate, Meditate

There are a number of styles of meditation. Find one that suits you and get into the habit of doing it at the same time each day. Ideally, the place you meditate should be comfortable, peaceful and warm. However, it is also helpful to catch a bit of down time at your desk or while sitting on public transport if you need to.

The following list contains some of the more well known forms of meditation. You will need to work with trained practitioners to learn them.

- Transcendental meditation – according to ancient Indian Vedic principles
- Sidha – according to Gurumaya – India
- Chi Gung – Chinese based
- Buddhist – breath and bliss
- Anthroposophical – according to Rudolf Steiner principles
- Stillness meditation – Ainsley Meares

To get your body into an optimum state for sleep, meditation, relaxation exercises and visualisation are useful tools. Find a tool that relaxes you and use it each night to help you let go of stress and tension.

Getting Started with Physical Relaxation

- Set aside a time each day to allow yourself to physically relax. Even 10 minutes a day will make a difference. Make it a daily ritual. It will be like a holiday each day

- ✦ Find a comfortable and quiet place where the telephone will not be heard or alternatively take it off the hook for the duration
- ✦ Breathe in and out of your nose allowing the exhaled breath to be of a longer duration than the inhalation. As you breathe, concentrate on relaxing each muscle from the top of your head all the way down to your body
- ✦ You can imagine or say to yourself:
  - My forehead is as smooth as silk, my eyes are like liquid amber
  - I am so relaxed that my cheeks are like putty, my jaw and mouth is soft and slightly open as my breath moves in and out like the waves of the sea
  - My shoulders are dropping towards my toes. All tension is evaporating and I feel peaceful
  - My spine is cocooned, as if sinking in sand
  - My arms are lying comfortably next to me as I focus on my breath
  - My ribs feel light and spacious
  - My pelvis feels in alignment
  - My upper legs sink into the softness and I let go of any tension that dwells in me
  - My lower legs are resting comfortably as are my feet, toes and the soles of my feet
  - I am at ease, in peace

Basic Meditation Technique

- ✦ Find a quiet place where you will not be interrupted and take the phone off the hook
- ✦ Sit upright in a comfortable chair with your feet firmly planted on the floor

- Begin by taking some long slow breaths-making the exhalation longer than the inhalation
- Focus your attention on the sound of your outward breath
- When external noises or unsolicited thoughts disrupt your concentration, acknowledge them, let them go and return your focus to your breath
- Begin by employing this technique for 5 minutes. Practice this each day for a few minutes longer than the previous day until you can meditate for 20-30 minutes
- Come back into your body by slowly becoming conscious of the sounds of your surroundings and wriggling your fingers and moving your feet
- Sit quietly and savour the quiet feelings and experiences from the meditation before resuming your activities
- Drink a glass of water to hydrate your body

Visualisation

Our imagination is a wonderful and exciting tool that we can harness to work for us in our daily lives. Visualisation is simply day dreaming with intent. It is a practice where the mind thinks in pictures.

It differs from meditation because with visualisation we need to remain alert and focused so that we can be responsive to our imagery whereas with meditation you let go of specific thoughts.

Visualisation enables us to make direct contact with our inner being, in order to manifest our desires into reality. The mind is brought into play to affect the body, and the way we negotiate and process emotions and experiences.

If you understand that what you think can manifest into reality, you can work towards turning around negative thought patterns and even create physiological changes.

The use of mental imagery is a way to clear out old negative patterns that we have outgrown and replace them with positive seeds that start to shoot new growth.

This practice forms a vital part of healing on all levels, giving us the power to take responsibility for our health and actively participate in it.

Seeing is Believing

When we enter into visualisation, it is important to clarify what it is we are striving to achieve. This creates space for the intent to begin the healing process as well as creating direction to initiate change. And it is important to be specific because you usually get what you ask for.

To begin, create a peaceful external environment that is free from disruption so that you can relax into the imagery. This means our external and internal environments mirror each other and facilitate a quiet mind.

The following exercises should be utilised before bed and practiced for 21 days in a row. The 21 days is significant as it parallels the natural biological rhythms present in all of us, most visibly women who are used to a cycle of three weeks of hormonal regulation. Psychologists believe it takes 21-30 days for the mind to absorb and process new thought patterns and hold them without rejection.

Preliminary Practice

This simple exercise will help you relinquish stress in your body and mind and prepare you for one of the following visualisations. It can be done while you are lying in bed or sitting in a chair in the lounge or garden.

Make sure that this is an uninterrupted time for you to relax. Allow your mind to be still, calm and open to the specific imagery.

Close your eyes. Breathe in and out until you feel relaxed. Take about 10 full breaths. The out breath should be longer and slower than the in breath.

Begin one of the following visualisations. Try each one to experience which resonates best.

Exercise 1   Reversing into sleep

One cause of insomnia is an inability to relinquish the energy of the day's events. The following exercise should be done only if the day has not been too stressful because it involves reliving everything that you experienced that day.

- Lie in bed with your eyes closed
- See yourself reliving the day's events in reverse order starting with the last event of the day and remember it as an image
- Go through each event until you are at the image of waking up in the morning
- It is appropriate to acknowledge each event and see what and how you would change and correct each one by having a different behaviour and attitude
- Give thanks for the day

Exercise 2   Visualising your perfect holiday

Do this visualisation in bed and begin with the preliminary practice as above.

- Imagine that it is midday and the sun is shining in the blue sky. You are lying on soft golden sand on the beach and the sand is like a cushion for your whole body. You feel warm and relaxed.
- Feel and see the waves lapping at your feet cleaning and clearing the soles of your feet

- With each gentle lapping of the sea water you feel more and more relaxed and the water washes away the build up of toxicity in your body as it is released through your feet
- After a few minutes you notice that it is now sunset and the sun dips and disappears
- As the sky turns dark see and feel yourself transported back to your bed feeling deeply relaxed and then asleep

Exercise 3   Falling leaf visualisation

This visualisation is helpful after a very stressful day.
- Start with preliminary practice.
- Imagine you are out in nature where there is a beautiful waterfall
- You decide to go and stand under it and the water is fresh but not cold
- See and feel the clear water cleansing you
- You feel relaxed as you then lie down on the banks of the waterfall
- Next to you are a selection of leaves. You pick up the first leaf and place your stress and worries inside it
- In each you place a different concern and allow the warm wind to blow them all away
- You then see yourself in your bed, warm relaxed and falling asleep

Painting a Happy Picture of Sleep

Art Therapy

Art has the power to touch us profoundly. It is a universal language that when used as a therapeutic medium, can be a path of development.

Art therapy is a creative essentially non-verbal therapy in which our inner experience such as our subconscious is outwardly expressed in images. It does not require artistic skill or talent as it is not a painting or drawing class per se; it is an activity that can help a person explore problems that may be hard to vocalise and it is a powerful adjunct therapy for dealing with anxiety, depression and other psychological and physical health issues.

The artwork is not the end result; the process and journey of discovery is the way to contact the inner voice.

Media such as photography, paints, crayons and modelling clay are employed rather than logic or cognitive understanding. These mediums bypass the mind's censors and allow spontaneous expression.

When painting is implemented therapeutically, the needs of the patient are met through the deep understanding of colours and their application. Some therapists also use wet paper to elicit a certain response from their patients.

Drawing in symbols is safe and not confronting. What appears on the paper can reveal deep feelings and issues such as when a person feels inwardly cramped and needs to expand or whether one is too dispersed and needs centering and quieting.

Unimpeded creativity in a safe environment allows us to fully participate in reconnecting with nature to find equilibrium and answers to the difficulties of mind, body and spirit. The creative process is connected with warmth, movement and openness. Warmth comes from both the activity and the opening of the senses where one feels release and joy.

In painting we experience movement. This change is evident on a cellular level and our pulse and breathing is altered through the creative process. Often a participant needs to remove their jumper because of the energy and heat created through the activity.

The therapist will guide the participant through a specific healing process using appropriate colours and various techniques to bring inner harmony and balance. It can take on the form of active meditation where crayons, paint, sand, clay and collage may be used together or individually to express inner experiences.

The act of putting paint or crayon on paper produces emotion. It is like working in another language and the understanding or the connection can come immediately or much later. Regardless, change is taking place at even deeper realms than our subconscious; it is also taking place at the cellular and spiritual levels.

Individual colours have a profound effect upon us, each 'speaking' to us in a different way, giving us nourishment and the ability to heal. The quality of the colours used, therefore is of paramount importance.

Like the breath, life is expansive and contractive. Likewise there are colours that are expansive and contractive. Yellow, orange and red are expansive colours that are lively, aspiring and exciting. Red can give us a new dimension. The heart is expanded and warmed with the glow of yellow.

Blues and greens offer peace and tranquillity. Blue is peaceful and cooling like water. It is a contractive colour that reminds us of shade, repose and melancholy.

Asthmatics may benefit by regulating the breathing through specific application of both expansive and contractive colours. For instance, they may benefit from placing blue on one corner of the painting going towards the middle of the paper and yellow on the other side, merging to green in the middle.

It is similar with sleep; an art therapist will help the breathing process if there is apnoea, sinus troubles, snoring or allergies using colours such as blues and yellows.

Those who find it hard to sleep for reasons of grief, trauma, anxiety, fear and other emotional upsets will find this a tremendously helpful adjunct therapy. They will be guided through creative expression to elicit a response either with paint (even finger painting), modelling clay or sand to create a cathartic effect in the mind and body.

Pictures are interpreted and understood on a metaphoric level. If you are ill you may draw that illness as you visualise it and work with it out there on paper instead of inside you. Used in conjunction with other therapies such as homoeopathy, flower essences, diet and lifestyle, it can help with the healing process as well as relieving any 'issues' you might have, which in turn will help you sleep.

As a modality to facilitate change and self-realisation, it can awaken creativity, free constraint, create awareness, solve problems, reveal unconscious material, be cathartic and work through conflicts. It encourages hope, promotes personal growth and creates equilibrium.

It is an excellent medium to use with children who usually are unable to express their feelings at a deep level. This gives them a voice in a safe medium.

Art therapy can be used in conjunction with any other therapy, both for children and adults and needs to be facilitated by a trained art therapy practitioner.

Caution

Art therapy is contraindicated for people with schizophrenia as it can cause their psyche to fragment even more.

Exercise

Any kind of exercise that you enjoy, that makes you feel happy, be it marathon running, gardening, trench digging or long distance vacuum cleaning will aid your ability to sleep well.

However, try not to exercise before bedtime as a drop in body temperature aids sound sleep. A gap of five to six hours between bedtime and exercise is best and better still is morning exercise.

Proof that Exercise Aids Sleep

A Stanford University Medical School, California, study assessed the impact of exercise on middle aged older people's sleep. Researchers looked at factors such as how long it took to fall asleep, total hours of sleep per night, amount of times they woke in the night, how people felt on waking, and how well they functioned during the day.

Participants exercised at least four times a week and twice a week they participated in an organised aerobics class, which included 30 minutes of endurance training. The other two times they exercised on their own, doing 40 minutes of brisk walking or riding and exercise bike.

Results showed that the subjects reported sleeping better when they added regular exercise to their routine and the improvement of physical health had a positive impact on the mind.

Exercise should be vigorous enough to create some sweat. Participants in the Stanford study did not report improved sleep until they had been exercising for 16 weeks, so make sure you stick with it.

Another interesting body of research carried out at the same university involves exercise and people not going into a sleep that they never wake up from.

What they discovered over a 20 year study of people between the ages of 50 and 72 was that regular runners have a 40 per cent less risk of disabilities and fewer incidences of diseases such as Alzheimer's and cancer. Results revealed that 34 per cent of the non-runners died prematurely compared with 15 per cent of the runners.

Life expectancy in the 50-70 age group is dramatically affected by exercise. It has been shown that mortality rates are three times higher in those who do not keep physically fit compared to those who do.

Yoga

The purpose of yoga is to restore the mind to simplicity and peace. The yoga poses, or asanas, are a harmonious and wonderful way to bring quietness to the mind and can be used to treat mental, emotional, physical and spiritual ailments.

Through the practice of yoga, the body and mind integrate and work in harmony. Energy that is otherwise dissipated through coping with stress and pain is now diverted to healing, rest and rejuvenation.

The following asanas can quieten the mind, encourage diaphragmatic breathing, soothe brain cells and calm adrenal glands. They open the chest and calm the breath. Because there is a huge relationship between the way we breathe and our state of mind, when the breath is calmed there is a flow on effect of the mental state.

Practicing yoga can place you in the perfect state for peaceful sleep. As a tool for treating insomnia, the poses must be sequenced in the following way for maximum benefit as each asana complements the next.

These postures are practiced with supports of one kind or another such as a cushion for back issues or neck supports. They are best applied with a yoga instructor so they can advise regarding proper practice as well as offering the appropriate props for physical support.

Here Come the Asanas

1. Supta Baddha Konasana

This posture opens the chest, releases the diaphragm and promotes deep steady breathing.

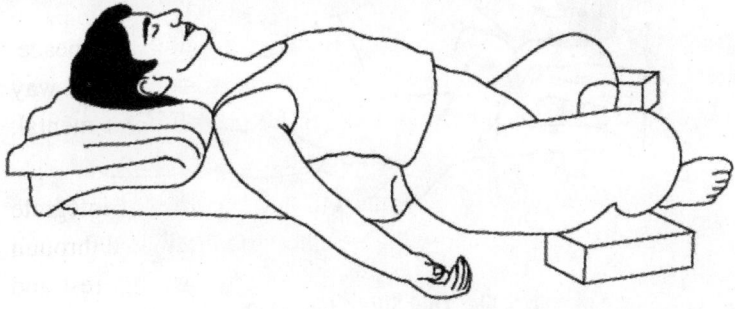

Fig. 16.2 *Supta Baddha Konasana*

2. Adho Mukha Virasana

This posture supports the front of the body, calming the adrenal glands, which regulate some of our hormones. It also relaxes the heart, reducing blood pressure and palpitations.

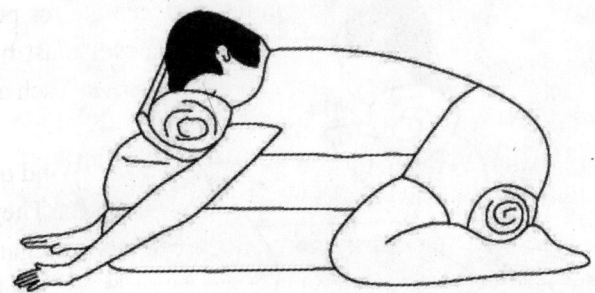

Fig. 16.3 *Adho Mukha Virasana*

3. Supta Virasana

Opens the chest, releases the diaphragm and promotes deep steady breathing.

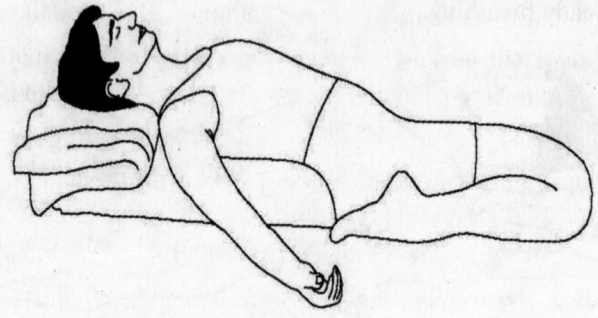

Fig. 16.4 *Supta Virasana*

4. Adho Mukha Virasana

Opens the chest, releases the diaphragm and promotes deep steady breathing. It is important after Supta Virasana (i.e. Asana No. 3) to repeat Adho Mukha virasana as it releases the back.

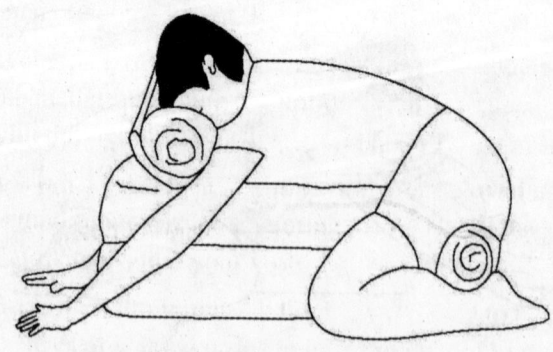

Fig. 16.5 *Adho Mukha Virasana*

5. Supported Utanasana

This rests the brain, quietens the senses and relaxes the heart.

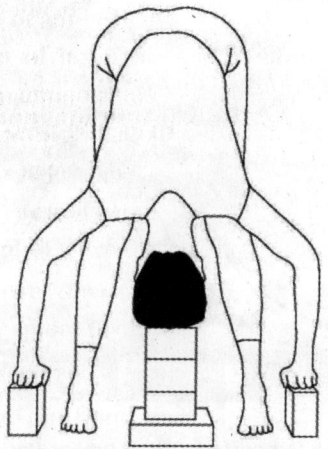

Fig. 16.6 *Supported Utanasana*

6. Supported Prasaritta Padotanasana

Rests the brain, quietens the senses and relaxes the heart.

Fig. 16.7 *Supported Prasaritta Padotanasana*

7. Supported Adho Muhka Vanasana

Rests the brain, relaxes the heart and balances hormonal flow.

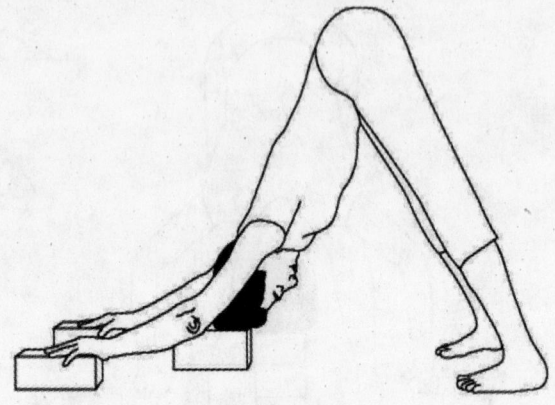

Fig. 16.8 *Supported Adho Muhkas Vanasana*

8. Sisasana

Only do this posture if you are an experienced yoga practitioner.

Relaxes the heart, balances hormonal flow and promotes health in all the body's systems.

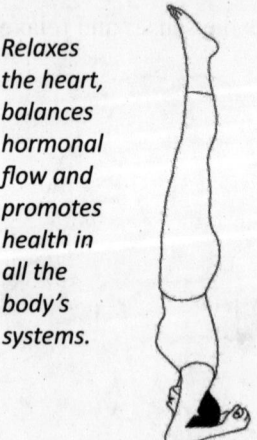

Fig. 16.9 *Sisasana*

9. Supported Janusisasana

Calms the adrenal glands, withdraws the senses and relaxes the heart.

Fig. 16.10 *Supported Janusisasana*

10. Supported Pachimotanasana

Calms the adrenal glands, withdraws the senses and relaxes the heart.

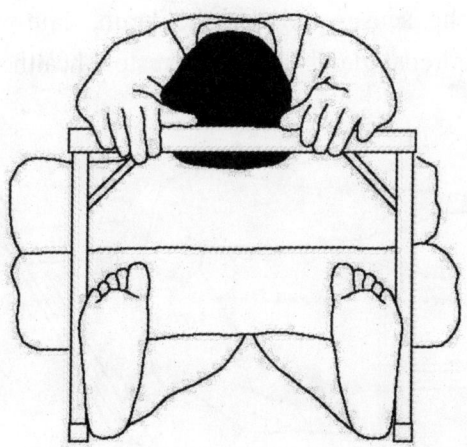

Fig. 16.11 *Supported Pachimotanasana*

11. Supported Saravangasana

Lowers blood pressure, promotes diaphragmatic breathing, relaxes the brain, calms the heart and helps restore health.

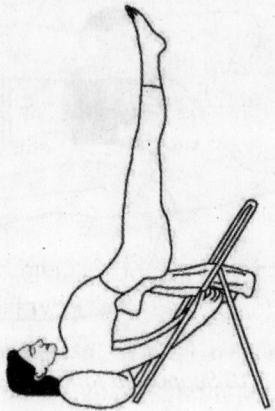

Fig. 16.12 *Supported Saravangasana*

12. Supported Halasana

Withdraws the senses, relaxes the brain, calms the heart, soothes the adrenal glands and helps restore health.

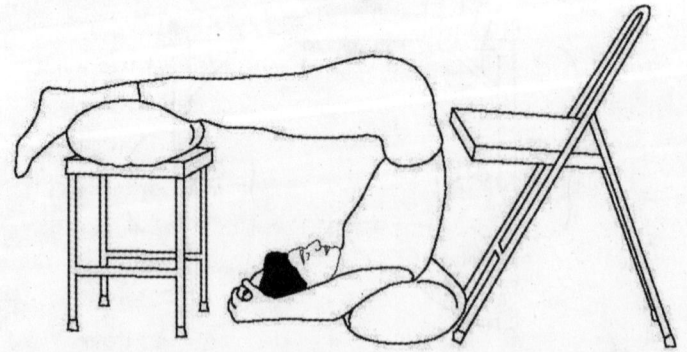

Fig. 16.13 *Supported Halasana*

13. Viparittakarini

Calms the mind by relaxing the heart.

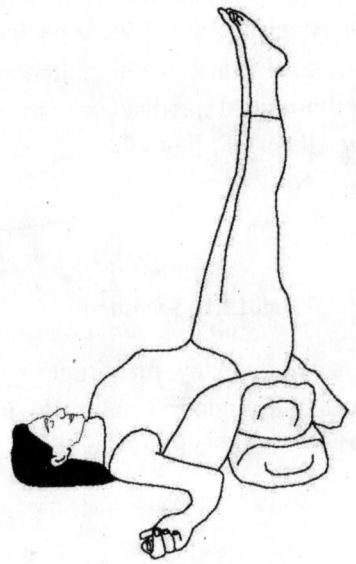

Fig. 16.14 *Viparittakarini*

14. Supported Setubandha

Calms the mind by relaxing the heart and slowing the breath.

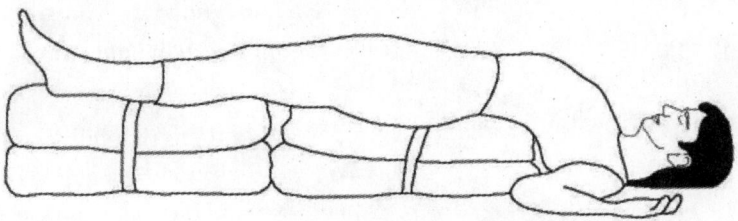

Fig. 16.15 *Supported Setubandha*

15. Savasana

Rests the body and mind as one and promotes health and healing by calming the body and mind.

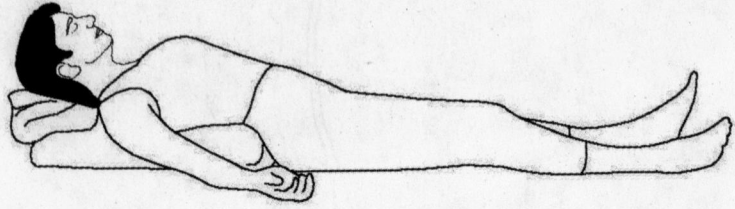

Fig. 16.16 *Savasana*

After a yoga session, many practitioners offer relaxation, breathing techniques and guided visualisation in case you were only on the outskirts of 'la-la' land by the end of the session.

Chapter 17

Put Away that Laptop and Get to Bed – Children and Sleep

*There was never a child so lovely,
but his mother was glad to get him to sleep.*

– Ralph Waldo Emerson

Are the Kids Getting Enough Sleep?

It is now quite common for children to have erratic sleep patterns and it is a constant concern for many parents. Research shows that children are generally not getting enough sleep and this results in a whole host of problems including:

- Poor performance in school
- Behaviour problems
- Daytime tiredness
- Moodiness
- Hyperactivity
- Hormone imbalances that increase the risk of obesity and diabetes

There may be a variety of reasons for disrupted sleep in children such as:

- Reluctance to go to sleep
- Lack of parental discipline when it comes to bedtime
- Equipment such as mobile phone, phone charger, computer and TV in the bedroom
- Waking in the middle of the night with nightmares
- Fear of darkness
- Food allergy
- Sleepwalking (not that common)
- Bed wetting, which can also affect some older children

Generally, children's sleep issues are relatively easy to fix.

Sleeping from Babyhood to Adolescent-hood

Although newborn babies sleep an average of 16-17 hours per day it is generally intermittent sleep. These irregular sleep cycles start to settle down after about six months when a routine is established and they do not need to be fed as often.

As babies develop, the total number of hours they need for sleep decreases. However, they do behave differently according to their individual needs, environmental influences and personalities. A six month old child may wake up briefly during the night, but it should only last a few minutes and then they should go back to sleep easily on their own. However, this is not always the way of things.

As they get older and become more aware of their environment (from 18 months – 2 years old) they are more likely to respond to external stimulus at bedtime. At this age they start to see themselves as individuals separate from their mother, and hence separation anxiety can develop which can cause added angst about bedtime.

Each age in the development of a child can bring sleep issues. When puberty hits, its a different ball game altogether because there are so many exciting reasons not to go to bed which can be a source of conflict between parent and child. It is important that parents set boundaries and make sure that their children go to bed at an appropriate time.

Tell a Phone

Now, here is an alarming situation. A recent Australian survey of 257 parents of 517 children found that almost 70 per cent of the children under 18 years of age had a mobile phone and 1 in 4 children of primary school age were allowed to take their phone to bed. A similar study in New Zealand in 2008 showed that 42 per cent of children between six and 13 years old had a mobile phone.

The awful consequence of this is that many kids spend their night texting friends till all hours of the night and morning. Of course this leads to serious sleep deprivation. Then, there is the issue of the radiation emitted from mobile phones. A growing body of evidence that is being denied and ignored by governments and populations shows clearly the strong connection between mobile phones and brain tumours, especially in young children.

This is not an isolated situation. Across the world it has become a norm for children from the age of six to be given mobile phones. Why they would need one is a mystery! The question here is; are we rearing another generation of insomniacs?

Fostering Good Sleep Habits in Children

The time to address sleep problems with children is not at bedtime; the process needs to start a couple of hours earlier. Just like adults, children need the regularity of bed and waking times to keep their body clock regular.

Here are some ways to make the lead up to bedtime a pleasant daily event to look forward to:

- Have a tea party with your child using chamomile tea, which will help them to relax. An hour before bedtime is best. Children over the age of seven can be given a single cup of either passion flower or skullcap tea at bedtime. (Check with a health practitioner to ensure the tea is appropriate for the individual child)
- Children over the age of 12 can be treated for insomnia with a single dose of the root of the valerian herb taken as a tincture or as tea just before bedtime
- For teenagers a combination herbal tea* is good. Combine equal amounts of valerian root and other herbs such as chamomile, passion flower and skullcap
- It is most important that a child feels secure and loved unconditionally. If parents are arguing or there are other tensions in the home then it would be no surprise to find that the child or children begin to have disrupted sleep patterns and bad dreams. The emotional and physical

---

*It is a good idea to rotate the herbal tea treatments so that the child is not drinking the same one each night. This will reduce the risk of them becoming tolerant to any of the herbs. So you might give chamomile tea for a few nights and then change to passion flower.

health of your child is one very good reason to deal with your relationship problems maturely

+ Reading to your children at bedtime is a lovely ritual that helps to strengthen the bond between you and your children Make sure that they are happy stories or meditation stories before sleep so that they feel relaxed and the dreams are sweet

+ Creating a prayer for or with your child imbues them with a sense of security. It could be as simple as giving thanks for all the good things that have happened in the day and looking forward to all the joy of tomorrow

+ Give the child a warm and relaxing bath before bed. (Refer 'Soaking in the healing waters' section, page 211)

A child's bedroom should be comfortable with a mild temperature

Lack of Sleep Weighs Heavily on Kids

A sleep study was undertaken by the US National Institute of Child Health, of children between the ages of nine and 12. They analysed the children's sleep times and compared them with their body mass index. Out of 785 children tested 18 per cent in the sixth grade were overweight and this was associated with less time spent in sleeping.

The same association was made for children in the third grade who were not getting enough sleep. They too were overweight.

What they concluded about children in sixth grade was that every additional hour sleeping made them 20 per cent less likely to be overweight.

Likewise, every additional hour of sleep for third grade children decreased the likelihood of obesity by 40 per cent.

The reason for this is that inadequate sleep disrupts the production of the hormones that affect weight such as insulin and leptin. The study concluded that having adequate sleep was one way to prevent children from becoming obese.

The researchers recommended that preschool children should have between 11 and 13 hours sleep and primary school children should have between 9 and 11 hours.

Children and Food Intolerance

Intolerance to any kind of food can cause a long list of symptoms; one of the first noticeable ones being that the child fails to thrive. The parent may not be able to put a finger on why the child is not thriving and one of the symptoms that presents may be sleep disruption.

Many parents may not be aware that their child is feeling anxious, irritable and restless at night because of what they have eaten during the day.

Children who are allergic or sensitive to dairy, wheat, corn and chocolate do not sleep because they are often troubled by symptoms derived from a compromised immune system. They can experience stomach cramps, itchiness, diarrhea, a racing heart beat and even cystitis.

The solution is to determine what the allergen is and treat it with either homoeopathic remedies and/or avoid the problem foods.

It is important to remember that the primary reason we eat is to nourish our bodies. When it comes to children, they are growing and developing on every level. What many people are not considering when they feed themselves and their children on foodstuff consisting of chemicals, colouring agents and carcinogens, is that they are setting them up to be plagued by all the illnesses that beset our modern culture.

Many of today's children are already obese and have clogged arteries. This is terrible. Eating good food not only affects our physical being, it also helps us to be and feel well, mentally alert and emotionally stable, and importantly, it does not keep us up at night.

CHAPTER 18

Aging Gracefully – Sleep and the Elderly

I want to die young at a ripe old age.

– Ashley Montagu,
Anthropologist and Humanist

The sight of a grandparent or elderly parent falling asleep in a chair during the day might not fill anyone with surprise because most people think that this is what happens when you get old.

And older people may have a similar expectation; that they feel tired a lot because it is just a symptom of old age.

This is a mistake. All things being, equal, an older person should feel fit and healthy and full of vitality. So, dropping off to sleep in front of the television is a sign that they are not sleeping well at night or perhaps that they are unwell.

There could be any number of reasons for this including snoring, apnoea, old habits of bad sleep patterns or a health condition.

Following is a list of complaints that can be associated with old age that may affect sleep.

- A need to urinate often through the night
- Chronic pain due to diseases such as arthritis
- Chronic diseases such as congestive heart failure
- Depression
- Neurological conditions
- Alzheimer's disease
- Organic brain syndrome
- Use of prescription drugs
- Lack of sufficient exercise
- Stimulation due to drinking too much caffeine

Of course, those who suffer from an illness need to address the management of their condition and symptoms with the assistance of their health practitioner.

Sleeping is an important element in the treatment regime because without adequate sleep our systems will find it hard to heal and rejuvenate.

Mature Sleeping Habits

Generally, older people require less sleep, and their sleep is less deep than that experienced by the young.

While illness can cause sleepless nights, having regular good sleep will also impact significantly on the well-being of the individual. Taking a holistic approach and examining all the possibilities to manage a health condition will pay off.

Otherwise, implementing good sleep hygiene will enhance the journey into and through a peaceful night's sleep.

Sleep hygiene tips for the chronologically challenged

- ✦ Maintain a quiet sleep environment
- ✦ Drink a glass of warm milk before bed. Best not to drink alcohol before bedtime as it will cause you to wake up during the night
- ✦ Take regular exercise
- ✦ Do not lay awake for long periods when you cannot fall asleep. Get up if this goes on for more than 20 minutes and read or listen to gentle music, then go back to bed when you are feeling sleepy
- ✦ The use of sleeping pills to promote sleep on a long-term basis can cause addiction. Try some of the herbal remedies recommended in this book, but check with your health practitioner first in case they interact badly with medications you are taking

How often do you hear people talk about the expectation of getting sick as they get older? People expect ill health and fear what they consider is inevitable. This kind of thinking can perpetuate ill health. Keeping your body and mind in shape and following good sleep hygiene goes a long way towards disease and insomnia prevention.

> *Sleep is the golden chain that ties health and our bodies together.*
>
> – Thomas Decker, Guls Home-Booke (1609)

Chapter 19

Recipes for a Good Nights' Sleep

Food for Thought

*All that we see or seem
Is but a dream within a dream.*

– DH Lawrence

Some foods keep you awake and some promote sleep. We know that it is best to eat a good meal at lunchtime and lighter meals at night. A heavy high fat meal at night will take a lot more digesting, which should not be occurring during sleep time.

Eat dinners that are high in complex carbohydrates with lesser amounts of protein. The right food may also depend on individual physiology and constitution. Some people find that seasoned and spicy food such as chilli, hot peppers and garlic can cause heartburn and make sleeping difficult.

The following types of evening meals will promote sleep providing you do not have sensitivity or allergies to any of these kinds of foods:

Ensuring that your daytime diet is rich in B vitamins will help you sleep; the B group supports the nervous system and aids dream activity.

Foods rich in B vitamins include:

- Green vegetables
- Nuts
- Dairy foods
- Soya beans
- Yeast extract
- Seeds
- Seafood
- Eggs

Slow burning carbohydrates such as oats, barley, rice and beans provide the body with a steady release of energy that helps keep the system on an even keel all day.

When Eating Before Bedtime is Ok

If you need to eat after the evening meal then try not to do so under one and a half hours before going to bed.

The following snacks will aid sleep:

Nighty Night Nuts

Eat a handful of walnuts as they are a good source of tryptophan which is the precursor to melatonin.

Sleepy Smoothies

It is easy to make a smoothie. Just put all the ingredients in a vitamiser and switch it on.

The following smoothie combinations are delicious and sleep enhancing.
1. Cashew and banana smoothie.
2. Almond and banana smoothie with either coconut, soy or organic cow's milk.

Shuteye Juice

Juice 2 stalks of celery and enough leaves of cos lettuce to make 1 full glass of juice.

A Date with Sleep

This drink is full of tryptophan.

Ingredients
- 1 cup of milk
- 2 dates chopped and pitted

Cooking method
- Place milk and dates in a saucepan.
- Simmer until warm.
- Eat the dates and drink the milk.

Yo Go Snooze Juice

Ingredients
- 1 glass of milk or yoghurt
- 1-2 tablespoons of brewer's yeast

Cooking method
Mix together well and drink.

Capricornian Dreaming
Ingredients
- Raw goat's milk
- 1 teaspoon of sunflower seeds or sesame seed butter
- 1 teaspoon of honey
- Slice of avocado

Cooking method
Blend all the ingredients to a smooth paste and enjoy the drink.

Bean to Sleep (Tomato Chutney with Baked Beans)
Ingredients
- 2 organic brown onions diced and fried
- 10 organic tomatoes or one can organic tomato paste
- 4 cloves of garlic
- ½ bunch of basil
- Handful of parsley
- 2 tablespoons of olive oil
- 1 can of organic cannelloni beans
- Herb salt to taste
- 1/4 cup of water

Cooking method
1. In a deep frying pan dice and fry brown onions.
2. Crush 4 cloves of garlic and add to onions.

3. In a saucepan plunge 10 tomatoes in boiling water for 2 minutes.
4. Remove and peel the skin of tomatoes.
5. Chop tomatoes roughly and add to diced and fried onions and garlic.
6. Add approximately ¼ teaspoon herb salt.
7. Chop basil and parsley leaves and add.
8. Add water and stir well.
9. Add more water if necessary.
10. Add 1 or 2 cans of beans and stir through.
11. To serve, warm up and serve on a good rye, soya or rice bread.

This will make enough for a number of containers that can be frozen.

Tomato Dozers

Tryptophan rich tomatoes are a good snack to have in the evening, provided you are not prone to arthritis as tomatoes belong to the nightshade family. Nightshades are bad for arthritic complaints. If not then try the following yummy snacks.

Snooze Stack 1

Tomato and turkey stack

(Turkey also contains high levels of tryptophan. This snack could be better than a sedative!)

Cooking method

1. Cut 1/2 a tomato in circular slices.
2. Place a slice of grilled turkey breast on top of the tomatoes.
3. Top with 3 or 4 slices of avocado.

Snooze Stack 2

Tomato and sardine snack with avocado

Cooking method

1. Cut 1/2 a tomato in circular slices.
2. Place sardines on top of the tomatoes.
3. Top with 3 or 4 slices of avocado.

Red Faced and Ready for Bed Soup

Tomato soup and rye bread
Serves 3 people

Ingredients

- 6 tomatoes
- 1/4 diced brown onion
- 1 clove of garlic chopped in 3 pieces
- 1 carrot chopped into small pieces
- 2 stalks of celery peeled and chopped in small pieces
- 1/2 orange sweet potato cubed
- 2 tablespoons coconut oil
- 3 basil leaves
- Salt to taste
- 3 cups of chicken stock (not salty) or extra light coconut milk or water

Cooking method

1. Plunge 6 tomatoes in a bowl of hot water and leave for 2 minutes.
2. Remove and peel skin.
3. Fry the onion and garlic in a saucepan.

4. Sautee carrots, celery and sweet potato and basil together.
5. Add tomatoes, chicken stock or any other liquid you wish such as soy sauce.
6. Simmer until all ingredients they become soft (approximately 30 minutes)
7. Add more liquid if desired, some fresh basil for a lovely aromatic flavour.
8. Cool the soup, then puree.

Sleeping Spears

Ingredients
- 8 asparagus spears
- Goats' chevre cheese

Cooking Method
Steam the asparagus spears and top with a small amount of goats' chevre cheese and season with salt and pepper if you need to.

Sesame Siesta Dip (Tahini Dip)

Ingredients
- 1/4 cup tahini (sesame paste)
- 1 tablespoon lemon juice
- 1 tablespoon olive oil
- 1/4 – 1/4 tablespoon of herb salt
- Water to thin the mixture into a paste as desired
- 1/4 bunch of flat parsley

Cooking method
1. Combine all ingredients in a blender.
2. Pour into a bowl and serve as a dip with julienne vegetables.

Nutty Napping Milk

Ingredients

- ✦ 20 almonds
- ✦ 2 tablespoons sunflower kernels
- ✦ 1 1/2 cups (12 fluid ozs) of water
- ✦ 1 cup rice milk
- ✦ Honey to taste

Cooking method

1. Blanch almonds in olive oil and blend.
2. Combine together with sunflower kernels and ¾ cup of water.
3. Continue blending.
4. Retain the rest of the water to be used later.
5. Blend at high speed until finely ground.
6. Strain into a jug through a fine sieve.
7. Return the remainder of the ground mixture from the strainer into the blender and blend again.
8. Mix rice milk with almond liquid and if necessary, add a little honey to taste.

Yoghurt N Coconut

Cooking method

1. In a small bowl place 4 or 5 tablespoons of yoghurt. Natural buffalo or goat's yoghurt is better than cow's yoghurt as it is less mucous forming.
2. Top with fresh coconut flakes.

CHAPTER 20

And It is Good Night from Us

Sleep on This

For people with sleep issues, night time can seem like a long and frustrating period. The ideas presented in Defeat Insomnia will hopefully be an impetus for you to begin a voyage away from frustration and exhaustion into a good, healthy balanced state of being.

Finding your solution requires information and intuition. Be guided by your inner knowledge to methods that resound with you.

Finding the right practitioners to work with to improve your health is very important. Make sure they are experienced with the issues that you are encountering and never be afraid to ask lots of questions. Knowledge gives you the power to make the right decisions.

There may be times when it is appropriate to use a range of natural therapies at the same time. It is important to find a combination that will enhance your chances of healing and prevent recurrence.

If you do not understand what a practitioner is doing or recommending, then say so. If you are not satisfied with the answer or if anything they do makes you feel uncomfortable you do not have to go on. You are in charge of your body.

Make sure you give your therapist the whole picture. A good practitioner will ask you everything about yourself, from your emotional state to lifestyle challenges and health problems; so do not hold back.

Also, it is vital for a practitioner to know if you are also being treated by a doctor and taking any pharmaceutical medication. And conversely, the doctor needs to know what remedies are prescribed by the natural therapist. If your doctor has no knowledge of or sympathy with natural therapies and herbs it might be time to find one who does; one important reason being that there is an inherent danger in taking pharmaceutical drugs and herbs without proper advice as they can in some instances interact adversely with each other.

If you are 50 and you have had a particular health problem and have not been able to sleep properly for 15 years then it is going to take a bit of time to heal; you can rarely expect the problem to disappear overnight. It has taken a long time for the condition to set in and a natural therapy approach is not like taking a regular pharmaceutical one where changes usually happen very quickly. And remember that although pharmaceutical medications for sleep are of course valid, the approach is a band aid one whereas most of the time natural therapies will help you weed out the cause.

Ask your health practitioner how long the treatment will take to work so you know what to expect. It may not always be possible to give an exact time frame because everyone is so individual but it is important to have a realistic expectation about the treatment and what can be achieved. This is where good and honest communication between patient and therapist is imperative.

One would expect there to be some positive shift after 6-8 weeks of treatment, or even sooner depending on the condition and how long you have had it. This also depends on how much you are willing to change and do for yourself.

Natural therapists are not miracle workers and sleeping well and getting well takes a concerted effort. That means you have to be involved in the process. If they provide herbal medicines and other lifestyle advice that you do not follow then do not expect the desired result.

Some therapies will be working in the background so to speak, and a range of changes will be taking place internally before the actual symptoms disappear. Make sure your therapist knows what you are experiencing.

There may also be times when a herbal approach is not appropriate or effective. For instance, if someone is very depressed or has a serious mental illness they may need to be treated with conventional medicines. Perhaps later they will be able to introduce natural medicines into their regime to enhance their well being.

Two people may suffer sleep onset insomnia, however, their reasons for experiencing it may be quite different. The natural therapist works to restore balance in the body rather than seeing a disease that needs to be healed. They will examine the person eclectically as a whole entity constituting mind, body and spirit.

This means that the problem is being dealt with profoundly, getting to the root cause of the illness in order to prevent recurrence.

The whole idea of healing is not to hand yourself over to the health care provider expecting them to heal you. This is disempowering. The idea is to come away with tools to empower you to manage your life and health. The natural therapist is there to help in an informed, compassionate and ethical manner. They are a conduit for change, which leads to healing and this is also facilitated through the dynamic interaction between patient and therapist.

So, if you have the need to sleep while at the wheel of your car as you drive home from work, make no mistake, you are sleep deprived and it is time to do something about it. Few people lead an optimum life. The very nature of the life we have constructed is in a constant state of flux so it is perhaps not reasonable to suppose that we will always sleep optimally.

Sleep is a vital ingredient in the health paradigm and it should be as valuable to us as exercising and eating the right food.

Let's face it, if you lived in a non-toxic environment and were getting the right balance of vitamins, minerals, nutrition, exercise, mental stimulation, sleep, joy and love there would be no need to write a book of this nature.

Unfortunately this is not the reality we live in so we have to work to improve our own circumstances using all the tools at our disposal; and prevention is the best medicine.

Remember what the wise sage Lao-Tzu said,
'A journey of a thousand miles begins with a single step.'

Sleep well!